LAND DISCARDED

State Alternatives for Planning and Management

A Task Force Report

The Task Force on Natural Resources and Land Use Information and Technology was sponsored by the Council of State Governments under a grant from the Resource and Land Investigations Program of the U.S. Geological Survey and in cooperation with the Office of Land Use and Water Planning, U.S. Department of the Interior. The contents of this report do not necessarily reflect the views and policies of the Council of State Governments or the U.S. Department of the Interior.

THE COUNCIL OF STATE GOVERNMENTS

THE COUNCIL OF STATE GOVERNMENTS
Lexington, Kentucky

Published April 1975 by
The Council of State Governments
Iron Works Pike, Lexington, Kentucky 40511

Printed in the United States of America

ISBN 0-87292-010-0

Price: $4.00
RM-549

Contents

The Task Force on Natural Resources and Land Use Information and Technology

James M. Dolliver, Administrative Assistant to the Governor, State of Washington, Co-Chairman

Honorable Gerald T. Horton, Georgia House of Representatives, Co-Chairman

Joseph Bodovitz, Director, California Coastal Zone Conservation Commission

Robert Cahn, The Conservation Foundation, Washington, D.C.

David Callies, Attorney, Ross, Hardies, O'Keefe, Babcock and Parsons, Chicago, Illinois

Dr. Charles H. W. Foster, Secretary of Environmental Affairs, Commonwealth of Massachusetts

Richard M. Heikka, Director, Tahoe Regional Planning Agency, South Lake Tahoe, California

Jonathan Howes, Director, Center for Urban and Regional Studies, University of North Carolina

Philip LaMoreaux, State Geologist, State of Alabama

Professor Philip H. Lewis, Jr., Director, Environmental Awareness Center, University of Wisconsin

Virginia Nugent, National League of Women Voters, Washington, D.C.

Arthur Ristau, Director, State Planning Office, State of Vermont

Earl M. Starnes, Director, Division of State Planning, Department of Administration, State of Florida

Honorable Andrew Varley, Speaker of the Iowa House of Representatives

Daniel W. Varin, Project Director

Foreword

In June 1973, the Council of State Governments created a Task Force on Natural Resources and Land Use Information and Technology, whose major purpose was to foster discussion and review of related problems and programs in these areas. A series of background papers on Land Use Policy and Program Analysis was published in late 1974 along with *A Legislator's Guide to Land Management*. This final report contains findings of the Task Force.

The Task Force report describes the difficulties involved in land planning and management in terms which permit better evaluation by political institutions. Some of the recommendations and alternatives offered by the Task Force extend beyond the "familiar" solutions. However, many of the views expressed are similar to those previously expressed by other agencies concerned with current problems which are intergovernmental in scope.

This comprehensive report should provide an invaluable contribution to understanding the complexities of land planning and management and the role of state governments in this field. Appreciation is expressed for support provided by the Resource and Land Investigations Program, U.S. Geological Survey, in cooperation with the Office of Land Use and Water Planning, U.S. Department of the Interior.

Brevard Crihfield
Executive Director
Lexington, Kentucky
The Council of State Governments
March 1975

Preface

In the fall of 1973, the Council of State Governments appointed a Task Force on Natural Resources and Land Use Information and Technology to study the institutional, technical, and financial problems which States encounter in using natural resource and land use information, and in establishing planning and management programs.

The 14 members of the Task Force represent the executive and legislative branches of state government, state and regional planning agencies conducting land management programs, academic institutions, and public interest groups.

The Task Force was appointed at a time when there had been at least three years of attention focused on potential national land use policy and planning legislation. During this period, many States established land use programs. The programs took a variety of forms and have established a new base of experience in dealing with the complex problems of land use, environmental protection, and development.

The Task Force examined state experience and evaluated the options available to States in establishing or strengthening land management programs. The Task Force reevaluated the federal role in land management and provided a state perspective for future federal legislation.

The Task Force used several methods to identify and evaluate choices confronting States as they formulate policy and implement land management programs:

(a) A National Symposium on Resource and Land Information held in Reston, Virginia, November 7-9, 1973. Approximately 200 participants, representing the executive and legislative branches of state government, federal agencies, interest groups and organizations, and the public, met to explore means of changing patterns of decision-making, obtaining the information needed for planning and regulation, building the institutions to conduct these activities, and the resulting implications for the States and the federal government. The symposium proceedings have been published by the Council of State Governments.

(b) The Task Force held seven working sessions over a one-year period ending in September 1974. These sessions were devoted to examination and discussion of key issues:

Intergovernmental relations;
Organization, management, and finance;
Critical areas programs;
Citizen involvement;
Manpower; and
Data needs.

(c) The State Services staff of the Council of State Governments and consultants prepared a series of working papers describing important problems, outlining alternative courses of action, and suggesting possible solutions for consideration by the Task Force. The findings, recommendations, and alternatives developed by the National Symposium and Task Force are summarized in this report to the States. The background papers are published individually in a *Policy and Program Analysis* series.

The activities summarized here were sponsored by the Council of State Governments in cooperation with the U.S. Geological Survey and the Office of Land Use and Water Planning of the U.S. Department of the Interior. Mr. Daniel W. Varin served as Project Director under an experimental arrangement through which he was employed by the Council for a limited period while on leave as Chief of State Planning for the State of Rhode Island. Mr. H. Milton Patton, Associate Director of State Services, and Mr. Robert D. Matthews and Mr. James L. Breithaupt of the Council's State Services staff provided staff support. Mr. R. Deane Conrad, Ms. Mollie Zahn, Ms. Brenda Mearns, Mrs. Mardell Horn, Ms. Charlotte Amburgy, Mr. Thomas Hauger, Ms. Anne D. Stubbs, Mr. L. V. Watkins, and Mr. Leonard Wilson of the Council of State Governments also contributed to the project.

Mr. Frank Schnidman, Mr. Quinn Hudson, and Mr. Anthony Neville provided consulting assistance on certain portions of the study. Mr. J. Ronald Jones, Mr. Olaf Kays, and Mr. Edward Imhoff of the U.S. Geological Survey, and Mr. Lance Marston and Mr. Michael Rudd of the Office of Land Use and Water Planning participated throughout the project.

The primary contributors, however, were the Task Force members who spent many hours in discussion sessions and individual review of reports and findings. Their various perspectives and experiences were vital to a broad examination of state government land management programs. In addition, many state personnel contributed information and insight, especially in the case studies on organization, management, and finance.

Occasional reference is made in this report to the national land use planning legislation considered by Congress during 1973-74. Although no land use legislation was enacted by the 93d Congress, the bills passed by the Senate and reported favorably by the House Committee on Interior and Insular Affairs represent the results of more than three years of extensive hearings, testimony, and revisions by Congress and its staff. These bills and the commentary of the Task Force on them may provide a basis for future federal and state action.

1. Reemergence of the State in Land Management

The complexity and interdependence of economic and urban growth in the twentieth century challenge the traditional assumptions about land. The land use problems which have resulted from applying old solutions to new realities require the States to redefine their role in land regulation. Before States fashion a response, a clear understanding is needed of how the problems in land use emerged.

Traditional Attitudes toward Land

Americans have traditionally viewed land as "a commodity to be bought and sold, used and depleted by its owner as he sees fit, with a minimum of governmental involvement or guidance."[1]

This attitude is a natural outgrowth of our history. The colonization of North America was largely fostered by English companies organized to speculate in land. These companies operated in a period when feudal tenure systems were fast disappearing from Britain and Europe, and individual ownership of land logically became the ideal of the colonists. By 1776, "the concept of fee-simple ownership of land was firmly established and nearly universal in the Colonies."[2]

Land tenure in fee-simple, limited only by the common law doctrine of nuisance, was well suited to an America in which development of land was an ideology of the society and the economy. Economic growth throughout the nineteenth and well into the twentieth century was primarily a matter of exploitation of resources — farming, lumbering, mining, and most other important economic activities depended directly on the land and its products.

Early Land Policy

Fear of foreign intrusion encouraged a policy of rapid expansion of the Nation across the continent and spurred legislation that made land ownership readily available to homesteaders and railroad builders. Through these policies, the original public domain (lands owned or held in trust by the federal government) dwindled from 1,442 million acres to 699 million acres.[3]

Governmental interests in land at the state and local levels in the first century and a half of independence were confined to recording deeds, collecting taxes, and enforcing the limited laws regulating trespass and nuisance.

As population grew, as economic activity shifted to manufacturing and commerce, and as small cities and rural trading villages grew into dense urban communities, the traditional concepts of land as a commodity and an infinitely available and durable resource were not questioned or tested. Instead, controls over land use, such as zoning, building codes, and subdivision regulations, were devised and applied in ways which insured that these concepts would survive. The limited governmental interest in land controls had been viewed as a proper expression of the public interest in land for, in keeping with the traditional concepts of land ownership, the public interest had been interpreted as the protection of property values and of the speculative potential of land. Economic, racial, and other forms of discrimination have been an almost inevitable by-product of this interpretation. These controls were exercised by local governments since, in the early twentieth century, they were commonly believed to be the governments best suited to deal with growing pressures on the land. State involvement was limited to the prerequisite enabling legislation for local land use regulation. The dual concerns for local regulation and for protection of the economic value of land were reinforced by the dependence of local governments on property taxes.

Fragmentation of Land Use Planning

With continued population growth and the transition of the economy from agriculture to manufacturing and services, the result of existing land use controls has been the protection of virtually unplanned development — not guided planned development.[4] Growth patterns which seriously abuse land and natural resources have occurred. Industry and commerce have been decentralized from older urban centers to outlying locations. Urban growth is haphazardly scattered throughout rural and undeveloped areas. Individual dwelling units use increasing amounts of land. As a result of the haphazard scattering of urban growth, housing and employment opportunities for the urban poor have decreased. There is burgeoning need for energy facilities, water, and waste disposal.

The traditional attitudes toward land and the governmental interest in it have functionally and organizationally fragmented land use planning. That planning which has been accomplished has often been directed to a single function or purpose with little reference to a framework of goals and with minimal consideration of the long-term consequences of decisions made on a case-by-case basis. Planning for a single activity is usually concerned only with the demand for facilities which support that activity and seldom considers the interrelationships of activities and the intensification of these relationships under urban conditions.

Planning which attempts to take a broader view of a number of functions and activities has usually been separated from those governmental institutions which could implement plans. Originally this isolation was seen as necessary to prevent compromising planning with politics. Local planning commissions were established as virtually independent boards, outside the regular governmental structure. Since neither executives nor Legislatures were responsible for these agencies, neither saw a need to be responsive to them. More recently, planning has been rendered impotent by division among levels of government. In an effort to create a regional perspective on areawide planning problems, planning responsibilities have been assigned to regional planning commissions, councils of local governments, or other multijurisdictional bodies. *At the same time, the authority to implement plans is almost always kept at the local level, resulting in the most minute concern taking precedence over the most widespread one if this is found necessary to protect some very localized interest.* Furthermore, while all States authorize their local governments to regulate land use, only a few require that their communities assume this responsibility. As a result, three fourths or more of the Nation's land is not subject to any land use controls.

Both the lack of attention to comprehensive planning and the failure to link plans and implementation have been exacerbated by most of the federal and federally assisted activities which deal with land:

> Federal grant-in-aid programs which call for a planning component and Federal procedures which license activities with significant land use impacts serve to reinforce, if not force, local single-purpose planning. Federal programs to assist State or local planning projects seldom bear implementation requirements; and, in the few cases where such requirements do exist, adherence is only infrequently required. Balkanization of land use controls is encouraged whenever Federal funds for planning are channelled past State and regional governments and down to the smaller jurisdictions empowered to conduct land use planning.[5]

Today, some 868 federal programs make available grants, loans, guarantees, technical assistance, land, or equipment, or authorize some direct federal action. Most are related in some manner to the ways in which land is developed and used. At least 137 of these programs have a direct impact on land use.[6]

The lack of comprehensiveness and coordination in land use planning has been accompanied by serious development problems and abuses of land and natural resources such as:

* Decentralization of industry and commerce from older urban centers to outlying locations;
* Haphazard scattering of urban growth throughout rural and undeveloped areas;
* Increasing use of land for each dwelling unit;
* Burgeoning needs for energy, water, and waste disposal;
* Problems and delays in finding acceptable locations for essential facilities which have particularly difficult impacts on natural resources and on other activities;
* Conversion of productive agricultural land and forests to other uses;
* Loss of open space and devastation of wetlands and other fragile resources;
* Construction in hazardous locations;
* Demolition of historic and architectural landmarks; and
* Destructive competition among communities for those land uses which pay high property taxes and which make few demands on public facilities and services.

The extensive failures of existing land use planning and regulatory measures to prevent or correct the problems and abuses listed above can be traced to several factors. The shortcomings of a concept of land ownership and the public interest in the private use of land which is not consistent with current realities are compounded by inadequate technical bases for decision-making and inept or improper administration of regulations.

The States have provided very little to their local governments by way of either financial or technical assistance, or direction in terms of statewide or regional growth and development objectives. Yet this assistance or direction is necessary if local governments are to use their planning and regulatory authority wisely and effectively.

Many of our current land use problems do not result from a lack of will at the local level, but stem from the fact that the scale and types of growth and change being experienced in many areas simply exceed the legal authority, the financial ability, or the territorial jurisdiction of most local governments.

Perhaps the most serious land use problem for a democratic society is that of territorial jurisdiction: local governments are called upon to make decisions which seriously affect people whom they do not represent, and whom they frequently do not consider or are not even aware of. In numerical terms, land use decisions which have a serious impact beyond the locality where they are made are a small proportion of all the actions taken; they have been estimated to account for less than 10 percent of the total. Their impact, however, is far more important than their numbers suggest.

Development and Finite Land Resources

The rapid emergence and increasing visibility of problems associated with land use and development have resulted in a growing appreciation of man's relationship to and dependence on his total environment. Combined with seemingly insoluble conflicts and endless obstacles in locating and constructing essential facilities for energy production and transmission, water supply, transportation, recreation, and other requirements of an urban society, they are bringing about a searching examination by the public and all levels of government of long-cherished beliefs about growth and about the rights and responsibilities of those who own land. The Task Force on Land Use and Urban Growth of the Rockefeller Brothers Fund finds that:

> There is a new mood in America. Increasingly, citizens are asking what urban growth will add to the quality of their lives. They are questioning the way relatively unconstrained, piecemeal urbanization is changing their communities and are rebelling against the traditional processes of government and the marketplace which, they believe, have inadequately guided development in the past.[7]

If this new mood is to prevail, land can no longer be seen as an economic commodity to be consumed as quickly as possible; instead, it must be considered a finite resource to be used sparingly. Further, the importance of the differing characteristics of land in determining how land should be used must be recognized. This new attitude toward land and the redefinition of public interest in land regulation have raised anew the taking issue and prompted States' interest in growth policy.

The Taking Issue

The proposition that land is a basic natural resource, and that the public has substantive interests in the ways in which this resource is conserved and utilized, challenges some long-established tenets and some persistent myths.

The Fifth Amendment to the Constitution of the United States protects a fundamental right with these words: "nor shall private property be taken for public use, without just compensation," a provision generally echoed and often strengthened or extended by state constitutions. But this brief phrase contains troublesome abstractions and ambiguities when it is applied to regulation of the use of private land in the interests of both the owner and the general public.

When is property "taken" by regulation — when the owner's exercise of full and complete dominion is restricted in any way, or limited severely, or when the land is completely removed from his control?

What is "public use" — enjoyment, or absence of nuisance, or physical occupation?

What is "just compensation" — does the securing of advantages to society as a whole and, therefore, to each individual and property owner, provide compensation which is just for some limitations on the use of land, or does any loss in value resulting from such limitations require monetary compensation?

The taking issue involves a balancing of individual and social rights and obligations. The efforts to achieve this balance through legislation and litigation furnish answers to the above questions — answers which may represent immutable principles or may simply reflect attitudes toward land which prevailed at various times in the past. The result is uncertainty as to what kinds of restrictions stop short of a taking and what kinds require compensation.

An exhaustive study of this problem, *The Taking Issue,* finds that "the taking clause is a serious problem wherever there is substantial pressure for urban growth, and particularly where the environment is sensitive." In addition, "the popular fear of the taking clause is an even more serious problem than actual court decisions."[8] The authors recommend five strategies for dealing with this issue which range from a complete departure from past decisions to accommodation with those stringent interpretations. These alternatives are:

- The courts could discard the idea that regulation of the use of land can constitute a "taking" by returning to a strict construction of the taking clause. Land use regulations would then be subject to the same standards of judicial review that are applied to other exercises of the police power.
- Land use regulations could be tested against the importance of the public purposes which they serve. The necessity of regulation would be balanced against the loss of choices of land use to the owner and the choices which he retains to determine whether a taking had occurred.
- Standards for determining when regulation constitutes a taking requiring compensation could be adopted through legislation, as has been done in England for many years. Courts have generally accepted legislative determinations in similar circumstances.

- Land use regulations can be more closely tied to "sound factual evidence" and be more carefully drafted. They should then be able to survive a court challenge under existing laws and interpretations.
- Compensation could be paid when necessary to counter a challenge to land use regulation, with or without extensive land acquisition programs to reduce the need for regulation. This would establish a middle ground between exercise of the police power and eminent domain through an administrative procedure for evaluating claims for compensation which allege an unconstitutional taking. Systems for transfer of development rights and payments therefor are an adaptation of this alternative.[9]

Resolution of the uncertainty which surrounds the taking issue is crucial in determining how the development and use of land can be successfully regulated.

Resurgent state interest in planning for land use and in managing natural resources is fundamental to an effective response to this situation. In the federal system, States clearly are the source of authority for exercise of the police power and the power of eminent domain in land use programs. The obstacles to use of this authority to solve or ameliorate current and future land use and natural resource problems can only be removed by the States.

State Growth Policy

Growth policy and land use planning are linked by the need to plan, within some realistic framework, for the demands which can be expected to be placed on land and other natural resources.

Knowledge of the amount of growth or change which may occur within various time frames is important to a planning process which attempts to manage resources instead of simply allocating resources to meet virtually unconstrained needs. The planning process will in turn provide a basis for formulation and evaluation of growth policy, since the process will define some of the limits of resource utilization.

Without an independent growth policy component, land use planning becomes open-ended in a situation of global industrialization and population growth, increasing human pressures on all physical and environmental resources, and rapidly increasing metropolitanization of population with the resulting altered distribution of population and economic activity. The total land area is viewed as two-dimensional space to be allocated among competing uses, primarily on the basis of economic and social utility, modified by political tradeoffs. The land use plans and zoning maps and other regulatory devices prepared over the past five decades have almost universally adopted this view, designating virtually the entire area involved for some type of economic or social use, and typically accommodating a level of population increase and economic activity several times greater than that which can be expected during any reasonable future time period.

States are responding to the new attitudes toward land and growth at both the policy and program levels. More than 21 States are attempting to set goals for future development. Fifteen States have joined together to organize the Southern Growth Policies Board to identify growth alternatives for that region. Six States have formed population commissions and 10 State Legislatures have adopted population stabilization resolutions.[10] Twenty-one States are undertaking statewide land use planning programs, and 8 have reached the regulatory stage. All States have some elements of land use control legislation directed to specific areas or problems such as coastal zone management, wetlands management, powerplant siting, surface mining, critical areas designation, property tax incentives, or floodplain management (see Figure 1).[11] All but one of the coastal States have applied for federal grants under the Coastal Zone Management Act of 1972 and most have begun planning and management activities.

Allocation of Responsibilities for Land Management

Increasing interest on the part of state governments in the process of developing and using land takes many forms, resulting in some significant changes in the distribution of functions which have characterized this field for the past five decades: new functions are being added at one or more governmental levels, and shifts of duties and responsibilities among levels is occurring.

Constitutional and statutory provisions affecting land, long-established practices in the way authority is exercised, and public views of property rights combine to make the determination of the most appropriate level of government for various policy-making, planning, and implementing responsibilities a complex problem in intergovernmental relations. (See Appendix 1: An Allocation of Activities to Levels of Government for Land Use Planning.)

A New Role for States

States must take the lead in bringing policies for the development and use of land into line with current economic and environmental realities and with the changing public attitudes which reflect these realities. The planning and regulatory procedures which have been in effect for five decades, authorized by the States and conducted by local governments in most cases, have not changed in response to changing needs and cannot serve contemporary concepts of the public interest in land management.

Some of the characteristics and attributes of land discourage change. Land has physical permanence. It attracts both vested interest and emotional attachment. It is surrounded by a complex legal structure. It is a basis of both private wealth and public tax revenue. It is a fundamental, if frequently overlooked, part of every human activity. All of these factors must be taken into account in redefining the appropriate activities of both States and communities in land management.

An increased state role in management of this resource will mean a modified role for local government; but this does not necessarily mean a diminished role. The weaknesses of the present system demand, instead, that the abilities of local governments to deal with issues of growth and development be strengthened, not

Figure 1
STATE LAND USE PROGRAMS*
(September 1974)

	Statewide land use planning & control (a)	Coastal zone manage-ment (b)	Wetlands manage-ment (c)	Power-plant siting (d)	Surface mining (e)	Designa-tion of critical areas (f)	Land use tax incentives (g)	Flood-plain manage-ment (h)
Alabama	P	—	—	—	yes	—	—	—
Alaska	—	—	—	—	—	—	—	—
Arizona	P	NA	—	yes	—	—	yes	—
Arkansas	—	NA	—	yes	yes	—	yes	yes
California	P	yes	—	yes	yes	—	yes	yes
Colorado	P	NA	—	yes	yes	yes	yes	yes
Connecticut	P	—	yes	yes	yes	—	yes	yes
Delaware	P and R	yes	yes	—	—	—	yes	—
Florida	P	yes	yes	yes	—	yes	yes	—
Georgia	P	—	yes	—	yes	—	—	—
Hawaii	P and R	yes	—	yes	—	yes	yes	yes
Idaho	—	NA	—	—	yes	—	—	—
Illinois	—	—	—	yes	yes	—	yes	—
Indiana		NA	we need	we need	yes	we need	yes	yes
Iowa	—	NA	—	—	yes	yes	yes	yes
Kansas	—	NA	—	—	yes	—	yes	—
Kentucky	—	NA	—	yes	yes	—	yes	—
Louisiana	—	—	yes	—	—	—	yes	—
Maine	P and R	yes	yes	yes	yes	yes	yes	yes
Maryland	P and R	—	yes	yes	yes	—	yes	yes
Massachusetts	—	—	yes	yes	—	—	—	—
Michigan	P	yes	yes	yes	yes	—	—	yes
Minnesota	P and R	yes	yes	yes	yes	yes	yes	yes
Mississippi	—	yes	—	—	—	—	yes	—
Missouri	—	NA	—	—	yes	—	—	—

we need →

State	a	b	c	d	e	f	g	h
Montana	—	NA	—	—	—	yes	yes	yes
Nebraska	P and R	NA	—	—	—	yes	yes	yes
Nevada	—	NA	yes	—	—	yes	—	—
New Hampshire	—	—	yes	yes	yes	yes	yes	yes
New Jersey	—	—	yes(i)	yes	yes	yes	yes	yes
New Mexico	P	NA	—	—	—	yes	yes	yes
New York	P	—	yes	yes	yes	yes	yes	yes
North Carolina	—	yes	yes	yes	—	yes	yes	yes
North Dakota	—	NA	—	—	—	yes	yes	—
Ohio	—	—	yes	—	yes	yes	yes	—
Oklahoma	—	NA	—	—	—	yes	yes	yes
Oregon	P and R	yes(j)	—	yes	yes	yes	yes	—
Pennsylvania	P	—	yes	yes	yes	yes	yes	—
Rhode Island	P	yes	yes	—	yes	—	yes	—
South Carolina	—	yes	yes	yes	yes	yes	—	—
South Dakota	—	NA	—	—	—	yes	yes	yes
Tennessee	—	NA	yes(k)	yes	yes	yes	—	—
Texas	—	yes	—	—	—	—	yes	—
Utah	—	NA	yes	—	—	yes	yes	—
Vermont	P and R	NA	yes	yes	yes	yes	yes	yes
Virginia	—	yes	—	yes	yes	yes	yes	—
Washington	—	yes	yes	yes	yes	yes	yes	—
West Virginia	—	NA	yes	—	yes	yes	yes	—
Wisconsin	P	yes	yes	yes	yes	yes	yes	yes
Wyoming	—	NA	—	—	—	yes	yes	—

*Indications that a State has a program in one of the above categories does not constitute an evaluation of the effectiveness of the program, nor does it indicate that the program is based on specific enabling legislation.

NA — Not applicable.

a. P indicates the State has a land use planning program under way. R indicates the State has authority to review local plans or has direct control.

b. State has authority to plan or review local plans or the ability to control land use in the coastal zone.

c. State has authority to plan or review local plans or the ability to control land use in the wetlands.

d. State has authority to determine the siting of power plants and related facilities.

e. State has authority to regulate surface mining.

f. State has established rules, or is in the process of establishing rules, regulations, and guidelines for the identification and designation of areas of critical state concern (e.g., environmentally fragile areas, areas of historical significance).

g. State has adopted tax inducements to withhold or delay development of open space (e.g., tax on present use, rollback penalty, contract between the State and landholders to provide preferential tax for commitment to open-space usage).

h. State has authority to regulate the use of floodplains.

i. Only in coastal zone area.

j. Partial.

k. Tennessee Valley Authority.

undermined. At the same time, the need to address problems which exceed the scale or scope of local governments must be recognized. The States are best suited to meet this need.

A brief review of some of the more important problems identified in the preceding discussion demonstrates the need for States to join local governments in building a new approach to land use issues, and provides some guidance for the evolution of a state-local management system. First, and basic to all other considerations, is the fact that the governmental powers which must be employed in resource management — the police power, eminent domain, and taxation — are powers of the State. Any use of these powers by local governments (in almost every case) depends upon a delegation of authority by the State. Use of these powers in new ways requires new delegations.

All of these powers are involved in the conversion of two-dimensional static planning and regulatory procedures into a resources management process which encompasses policy-making, planning, and implementation. The extension of this process beyond the traditional consideration of economic and social utility to include the natural and man-made characteristics of land and their impacts upon land use decisions requires that all of these powers be used in new ways. Replacement of long-established methods for allocating land to meet virtually unconstrained demands by a management process which balances these demands against the limitations of a finite and varied resource requires a degree of leadership and a technical basis that States must help provide.

States are also the logical units to assume responsibility for issues of greater than local concern: those problems which transcend the legal authority, the financial capability, or the territorial jurisdiction of a single community. This extension of the decision-making process to include all of those who would be significantly affected by a decision, or who would be expected to share in its cost, has generally not been achieved by the areawide arrangements devised for most metropolitan or rural areas. The jealously guided prerogatives of some localities will not be easily yielded. Actions by the States to create statewide or areawide mechanisms for handling those few decisions of broad concern are essential.

Many of these areawide decisions are being made in an ad hoc manner, giving little voice to local governments and shielding the decision-making process from public scrutiny. Transportation facilities, utility systems, major recreation areas, and other important determinants of development patterns are too often designed and constructed without reference to local land use plans or any larger comprehensive framework of policies or plans for growth and land use. An enlarged state role in land management could increase the ability of localities to influence these decisions.

Any new land use programs at either the state or local level will soon encounter the taking issue and its real and imagined limitations on land management processes. This is certainly an issue which must be addressed by the States. The alternative strategies outlined previously in this chapter must all be pursued either initially or solely at the state level, whether they involve a more precise determination of the point at which regulation constitutes a taking by the Legislature, a more restrictive construction of the taking clause by the courts, a broader definition of the basis or necessity for management, or compensation for loss of some potential use. Even the use of better evidence to support regulation will probably involve States, since they will have to supply much of this information.

Major Issues

State planning and management programs for land use and natural resources have taken a variety of approaches. These can be grouped into four general methods:

1. Statewide, comprehensive land use management.
2. Management of selected activities according to functional criteria.
3. Management of specific geographic or critical environmental areas.
4. Management of uncontrolled areas.

The particular technique or combination of techniques which States choose reflect their own needs and objectives. Regardless of the method used, major issues must be reconciled.

The Task Force has identified the most important of these in six problem areas:

1. Intergovernmental relations;
2. Organizing, managing, and financing the program;
3. Involving the public in the planning process;
4. Conducting critical areas programs;
5. Identifying and meeting manpower needs; and
6. Determining what data is needed and obtaining adequate information.

Each of these problem areas relates to and impacts upon all of the others. None can be considered in isolation. The difficult questions of allocating responsibilities and powers among levels of government, and of structuring the interaction between levels which must result, pervade any effort to improve management of land and natural resources. Once these issues have been addressed and resolved, States can begin to shape the mechanisms which they need to play their role in the intergovernmental process of land and resources management.

Few if any States will find that the existing structure of agencies and their functions meet their needs. States must then decide how to organize, manage, and finance these new activities.

Determination of methods for involving the public in managing land use and natural resources must be an integral part of the development of organizational and management tools. Public participation can be built into every important aspect of the management process only by providing for this participation when the process is developed. Effective public involvement must also be funded. These issues were separately defined by the Task Force to insure that they do receive adequate attention. In practice, however, they cannot be separated from the organizational, management, and financial questions.

The three remaining problem areas flow largely from these more basic topics. Critical areas programs are only one method of carrying out state land use and natural resources management programs, but most programs established thus far have used this technique in some way. Manpower and data needs must be derived directly from the allocation of responsibilities, the organizational and management approaches selected, and the methods to be used to involve the public. These areas also present their own interrelationships. As an example which is frequently overlooked, public participation in any meaningful form requires both staff and financial support.

The findings and recommendations of the Task Force in each of these problem areas are presented in the following chapters.

2. Intergovernmental Relations

Introduction*

The renewed interest in the responsibility of state government for land use planning and management is, in large part, an expression of concern for a lack of adequate intergovernmental action, and an absence of mechanisms for such action in this field.

Much planning for and regulation of land use and development takes place at the local level. As a result, the essential local considerations may be taken into account in the decision-making process, but broader considerations are often omitted. In the face of a growing inability of local governments to deal with growth and development which transcend the geographic scale and functional scope of local government, the decision-making process has become even more localized, frequently focusing on a neighborhood, a subdivision or, in its most restrictive form, on abutting property owners. Large-scale land use conflicts increasingly have been resolved by ad hoc solutions under crisis pressures.

Current efforts can then be seen in part as directed to reform of the institutional arrangements for planning and regulating the use of land. Much of this reform must be concerned with a redistribution of activities, a recognition of the need to bring factors of other than local concern into the planning process, and inclusion of all those who are significantly affected by development decisions to play a role in making those decisions. In short, a different balance of actions by all levels of government is needed than that which now exists.

The Task Force considered the following questions to be of paramount importance in the reform of intergovernmental relations in the land management process:

1. To what extent, if any, should state governments supplement or replace their political subdivisions in exercising state constitutional authority to control land use?

2. How can broadening of development considerations be reconciled with the concept of local home rule?

3. How can questions of more than local concern be identified?

4. How can state activities with profound effects on land use be coordinated and rationalized?

5. How can the significant federal interest, as expressed by both development and environmental programs and ownership of land, be recognized?

An effective response to these issues involves a redefinition of the roles and responsibilities of all levels of government, and strengthening of the linkages between levels.

The redefinition needed does not necessarily involve a radical departure from either past history or current concepts. Land use planning and regulation of

---

*For more detailed discussion, see Land Use Policy and Program Analysis Number 1, *Intergovernmental Relations in State Land Use Planning* (Lexington, Kentucky: The Council of State Governments, September 1974).

development have always been to some extent an intergovernmental activity. While virtually all of the preparation and administration of land use plans has been by local governments, an authorization to undertake these activities in the form of state enabling legislation has always been required. States in turn were encouraged to delegate these responsibilities to their political subdivisions by federal actions such as the publication and promotion of model enabling legislation for local planning and zoning boards during the 1920s.

Subsequent developments have also had intergovernmental impacts. The federal government has encouraged and funded local action in such basic land development programs as public housing and urban renewal. The HUD 701 comprehensive planning assistance program, which originally supported planning for small communities, has been expanded to support larger cities, counties, metropolitan and nonmetropolitan areas, councils of governments, States, Indian tribes, economic development districts, federally impacted areas, disaster areas, and interstate agencies. States have also extended their land use related activities, although not as rapidly or as dramatically as the federal government. Metropolitan park districts, financial aid to urban renewal projects, and housing finance authorities are examples of the growing state participation in programs directly related to land use.

More recently, local governments have joined to form metropolitan or regional planning agencies and have created councils of local governments, both usually under state authorizing statutes. States enter into interstate compacts or participate in multistate regional organizations in efforts to deal with similar problems at a different scale.

These efforts stemmed not so much from a failure of local government as they did from the increasing complexity of an urbanizing society and its broadening and increasingly destructive impacts on land use. From one perspective, all of these actions can be seen as preempting local prerogatives. Even the acceptance of federal funds to support local planning carries with it requirements which impinge on complete local autonomy. From another perspective, these same actions can be viewed as part of a continuing evolution in the intergovernmental partnership which the three-tiered federal structure represents.

State-Federal Relationships

The entry of state governments into a significant role in land use planning will create a whole new series of state-federal relationships. Many of these could spring directly from national land use policy legislation, but some are taking shape well in advance of such legislation. These are normal and reasonable responses to the growing interest of both levels of government in such issues as growth policy, urbanization, food supply, and environmental protection.

Federal Grants and Other Assistance Programs

The federal government provides a wide range of assistance to state and local governments, educational and other institutions, businesses, families and individuals, nonprofit associations, and others. *The Catalog of Federal Domestic Assistance* (1973 edition) lists and describes 868 programs which make available grants, loans, guarantees, technical assistance, land or equipment, or which authorize some direct federal action.

Many, if not most, of these programs are related in some manner to the ways in which land is developed and used, and at least 137 programs have a direct impact on land use. This group excludes those programs which provide financial support to land use or facility planning; it includes only those activities designed to stimulate the use of land for a specific purpose, such as through construction of buildings or public facilities or through conservation and protective measures.

The number of these programs, the wide range of activities which they support, and the number of federal agencies involved, present a significant problem in intergovernmental relations to States which are attempting to formulate and administer land use programs. The scope of activities involved gives some idea of the complexity of the coordination problem.

• 53 programs promote the construction or improvement of housing, from single-dwelling units to entire communities. Several programs are directed to specific areas: core cities, the urban fringe, and rural farm and rural nonfarm housing.

• 19 programs support use of land for recreation, agriculture, forestry, wildlife, or other open space uses through conservation of soil, water, and plant materials, and other protective measures.

• 8 closely related programs are oriented to prevention of floods and erosion, stabilization of shorelines, and other protective measures, regardless of the intensity of use of the area concerned.

• 5 programs assist the construction or extension of utility systems and services required to support intensive land use.

• 17 programs provide similar support for transportation systems of all types.

• 9 programs are designed to stimulate economic development: in general, minority business, rural area, and other specific types.

• 20 programs support construction or rehabilitation of community facilities for health, educational, cultural, and other purposes.

• 6 programs facilitate transfer of land from federal to nonfederal ownership.

This summary is incomplete since the 1973 *Catalog* omits such major and still active programs as the economic development assistance activities of the Department of Commerce; nor are new programs such as acquisition of estuarine sanctuaries under the Coastal Zone Management Act of 1972 included. However, this tabulation of the programs being administered by various cabinet departments and independent agencies is adequate to illustrate the difficulties which will be encountered in coordinating federal activities directly related to land use.

The Project Notification and Review System established by Part I of Office of Management and Budget Circular A-95 (discussed later in this report) provides a means of coordination for some of these programs. However, only about one half of these programs, or 67 of 137, are subject to review by state clearinghouses under this requirement, while a few more come under Part II of the Circular, which requires that States be notified of several direct federal development actions.

Three federal grant programs are so closely related to land use planning and management at the state level that they are briefly summarized here. These are the comprehensive planning assistance (701) program, the rural development program, and the coastal zone management program.

The comprehensive planning assistance program. Established by Section 701 of the Housing Act of 1954,[12] the initial purpose of the program was "to facilitate urban planning for smaller communities lacking adequate planning resources." Grants were made to state planning agencies, since the planning was to be done for rather than by the smaller communities, defined as those with a population of less than 25,000.

Through a series of legislative amendments and administrative actions, the 701 program has become the basic federal grant program for most planning agencies. The list of eligible recipients has grown to include localities of all sizes, counties, metropolitan and regional planning agencies, councils of governments, States, specialized agencies such as transportation planning organizations, interstate agencies, and Indian tribes.

Most of the planning activities funded through the 701 program during its first 10 to 15 years of operation were concerned with physical planning or closely related matters: inventories of land use and other existing conditions; population and economic base analysis; plans for land use, community facilities, circulation, and recreation; and preparation of zoning ordinances, subdivision regulations, and capital improvement programs. The more recent history of the 701 program has seen movement in two directions. The first has been the inclusion of requirements for specific planning activities, beginning with an "initial housing element" in 1969 and then extending to equal opportunity considerations and environmental impact assessment. The second has been to broaden the program into a planning and management effort designed to assist chief executives at all levels to identify problems in a wide range of areas, formulate policies and programs, implement them, and evaluate their effectiveness.

The Rural Development Act of 1972. This act establishes a mechanism for utilizing a series of programs designed to facilitate the development of rural communities through grants, loans, and technical assistance in employment, income, population, housing, and quality of community services and facilities.[13]

The rural development program can include a number of components dealing with housing, industrial development, water supply, sewage disposal, and others as necessary to meet the needs of a State or a substate district. The research, extension, and community service capabilities of institutions of higher education, and particularly of the land grant colleges, are identified as a major resource.[14] However, no funds are available through this program for development planning for rural areas. In addition to state and local resources, the 701 program and other federal grant programs and revenue sharing allocations are suggested for this purpose.[15]

The coastal zone management program. Established by the Coastal Zone Management Act of 1972,[16] the act declares the national policy to be to "preserve, protect, develop, and where possible, to restore or enhance" the resources of the coastal region by encouraging States to prepare and implement management programs for these areas. Federal agencies whose actions affect coastal areas are directed to cooperate and participate in these efforts.[17]

A grant program established under the act is administered by the National Oceanic and Atmospheric Administration of the U.S. Department of Commerce. The program is divided into two phases. During an initial period, not exceeding three years, grants are made to assist States to develop management programs, including delineating coastal zones, determining the uses of land and water to be permitted in this zone, designating "geographic areas of particular concern" and designating uses to be given priority, and setting up an organizational structure and mechanisms for implementing the program. Following approval of a management program by the Secretary of Commerce, a State is eligible for grants to assist in administering the program. Public participation is required, and the use of regional agencies and local governments in preparing and implementing the program is encouraged.[18]

Environmental Regulatory Programs

Three federal laws establish environmental regulatory programs which are of particular interest in guiding the use of land. These are the Federal Water Pollution Control Act, [19] the Clean Air Act, [20] and the Noise Control Act. The first two are also administered by the Environmental Protection Agency, while EPA and the Federal Aviation Administration are both involved in the pertinent sections of the third.

The Federal Water Pollution Control Act. This act was amended in 1972, replacing the Water Quality Act of 1965 and subsequent amendments, with a new approach to water pollution which bases enforcement actions on effluent limits rather than ambient quality. The 1972 act extends federal and state regulation to all navigable waters, requires specific effluent standards for treatment and disposal facilities which are to be enforced through a permit system, authorizes effective federal standards for toxic discharges, and strengthens both federal and citizen enforcement procedures.[21] The federal grant program for municipal treatment plants is expanded, and the federal share of project costs is increased.

Both the objectives and the planning activities of this act have serious implications for land use planning. The objectives mandate a new spatial relationship between economic activity and municipal wastewater collection and treatment systems. Locations will be selected for industrial facilities under constraints which did not exist in the past. The agency which decides where sewers will be located or extended is also deciding, to a considerable extent, where industry will locate. Since industry in turn often influences the distribution of housing and other related activities, municipal and regional sewage treatment authorities are in effect making decisions which significantly affect the total pattern of urban development.

Planning activity under Section 208, which overlaps the other levels by a large margin, involves even more direct land use considerations. Some federal and state officials view Section 208 as a national land use planning act. The planning activities undertaken under Section 208 include programming of the sanitary and storm-water collection and treatment facilities needed for a 20-year period. But the key linkage to land use planning lies in the requirement that the planning agency develop and implement a regulatory program that can control the location and construction of any facility that may discharge wastes.[22] These could conceivably range from an industrial plant to a parking lot with storm-water runoff to a water body.

The Federal Water Pollution Control Act will certainly result in an expansion of planning activities and a proliferation of agencies involved. No mechanism is provided to insure that the decisions made through these procedures will be consistent with each other or with any overall state policy on the development and use of land. There is no certainty and little probability that the development patterns which these decisions on waste treatment facilities will promote will conform to the more comprehensive land use plans prepared at any level.

The Clean Air Act. This act establishes a federal-state program designed to achieve national standards of air quality which protect public health (primary standards) by 1975. More stringent standards necessary to protect aesthetics, property, and vegetation (secondary standards) must also be achieved within a "reasonable time," to be determined by EPA.[23]

Although all States are required to prepare plans for implementing all of the air quality standards which EPA has adopted under the act by the statutory deadline, three aspects of these plans have the most significant implications for land use planning. These are complex source regulations, nondeterioration provisions, and transportation control strategies.

The first of these implements those provisions of the act which control the location of major new sources of pollution. Uniform performance standards have been set for many of the problem facilities for use in determining whether these facilities can be located in any area, depending on their impact on air quality. But since these procedures have been found inadequate to maintain air quality (through litigation), States are now required to approve in advance the location of facilities designated as "complex sources" — shopping centers, amusement and entertainment facilities, highways, and airports are the most typical examples.

These manifestations of the Clean Air Act will certainly affect the location of many activities which represent major land uses in themselves and which strongly influence the distribution of other activities which are not directly regulated under this act. Although more experience is required to evaluate the effects of these regulations, there is certainly some inconsistency in the directions which they imply. Their results may well be to force decisions on land use and development which are in direct conflict with state land use policy and with state, regional, or local land use plans. No mechanism has been provided to resolve such conflicts, other than to forego development.

The Noise Control Act. This act provides for coordination of federal research and other activities in noise control and authorizes EPA to set noise emission standards for construction and transportation equipment, motors and engines, and electrical or electronic equipment.[24]

Section 7 of the act deals with aircraft noise and its control through both application of noise standards to equipment and through airport and flight operating procedures. The second aspect is of most concern to land use planning since the pattern of land uses around airports is the primary cause of complaints about aircraft noise.

Procedures are established for coordination between EPA and the Federal Aviation Agency in measuring aircraft noise and in controlling and reducing its effects. Through amendment of earlier legislation, these procedures are tied to the certification of both aircraft and airports by FAA.

Existing Coordinating Mechanisms

By and large, those federal programs which affect land use most significantly are not well coordinated at the state level. The natural tendency to assign these responsibilities to operating agencies on the basis of their subject matter has generally been encouraged by the federal administering agencies, so that these activities are often dispersed throughout the governmental structure. Frequently, no central mechanism has been established or designated to coordinate the actions of these agencies or to insure that their activities are consistent insofar as they influence land use.

Two existing mechanisms for coordinating federal, state, and local activities enter into consideration of the intergovernmental relationships necessary for state land use planning. These are the review procedures required by Circular A-95 and the Integrated Grant Administration Program. Both mechanisms were initiated by the Office of Management and Budget. The latter is now administered by the General Services Administration and the former is managed by the Federal Regional Councils.

EPA has recognized the significant influence which its programs have on land use. A new agency has been established to coordinate the land use aspects of air, water, and even solid waste programs. The new agency will begin operation early in 1975. Its importance is indicated by its placement within the Administrator's office. EPA has also published a general policy statement on land use as it is affected by environmental regulations.

Interstate Relationships

Land use issues often transcend state boundaries. Major developments influence land use patterns which extend into adjoining States. Pollutants discharged into a stream in one State flow into other States. Economic difficulties in some regions of the country cause large numbers of people to relocate in other regions where jobs are more plentiful or better paid. Metropolitan areas frequently extend across state lines, some contain central cities located in different States, and a few are international. None, however, are governed on an interstate basis. Resources may be extracted in one State or region, processed in a second, manufactured into finished products in a third, and consumed throughout the entire country and a large part of the rest of the world.

The resulting land use problems add another layer of intergovernmental consideration to the process of planning for and regulating development. But the principle involved is the same as that expressed as the basic reasons why this process must be reformed. Just as some land use issues are of more than local concern and require state action, so are some of more than state concern and require interstate action. For obvious reasons, the interest in institutional reform at the second level has not paralleled that at the first.

Multistate Regionalism

Formal arrangements for joint or cooperative action by the States are made through interstate compacts or through interstate agencies. In the first instance, the States concerned take the lead in formulating compacts, which must be approved by Congress. In the second case, agencies are established by legislative or executive action (or both) for more or less standard operations throughout the country.

Interstate compacts are designed to meet specific needs or to carry out designated functions. They do not provide a general model for interstate organization for land use planning although some, such as the Tahoe Regional Planning Agency, could serve as a prototype for agencies created through this approach, and HUD 701 funds can be used to assist agencies created by compact in land use planning and other activities. There are also at least three of the more general types of regional organizations which can provide a starting point for interstate organization and action.

Regional Action Planning Commissions. Seven regional action planning commissions have been established under Title V of the Public Works and Economic Development Act of 1965. They were designed to develop long-range, comprehensive economic development programs, to coordinate federal and state economic development activities, and to promote increased private investment. Regions are designated by the Secretary of Commerce and commissions are formed by joint action of the Governors concerned and the President.

River Basin Commissions. River basin commissions are established under

Title II of the Water Resources Planning Act of 1965. They serve as the principal agency for coordination of governmental and private plans for the development of water and related land resources. They are responsible for preparation and maintenance of comprehensive plans which provide a framework for coordination and for determination of priorities and scheduling of projects. The commissions are created by the President upon request of the States concerned and after approval by the Water Resources Council.[25]

Federal Regional Councils. A Federal Regional Council has been established in each of the 10 standard federal regions by Executive Order Number 11647 (February 10, 1972). The purpose of the councils is to improve the administration of grant programs by improving program operations, developing funding programs in cooperation with state and local officials, and encouraging joint and complementary grant applications.

State-Local Relationships

In theory, land use planning should present no serious problems to the States in their relationships with their local governments. Regulation of development is just one of many areas in which the State is sovereign, and the principle which views local governments as creatures of the States in such situations has long since been established. The U.S. Supreme Court has stated this rule broadly.

> Neither their [local government] charter, nor any law conferring governmental powers, or vesting in them property to be used for governmental purposes, or authorizing them to hold or manage such property, or exempting them from taxation upon it, constitutes a contract with the state within the meaning of the Federal Constitution. The state, therefore, at its pleasure may modify or withdraw all such powers, may take without compensation such property, hold in itself, or vest it in other agencies, expand or contract the territorial area, unite the whole or a part of it with another municipality, repeal the charter and destroy the corporation. All this may be done, conditionally or unconditionally, with or without the consent of the citizens, or even against their protest. In all these respects the state is supreme, and its legislative body, conforming its action to the state constitution, may do as it will, unrestrained by any provision of the Constitution of the United States.[26]

In practice, the situation is by no means as simple as the decision quoted here would imply. There is a significant difference in land use planning and regulation, as in many other areas, between what a State may do, and what it can actually do, in dealing with its local governments. This is reinforced by a traditional view, beginning at least with the regulation of nuisances early in this century, that the use of land is a local concern.[27]

The system of land use planning and control of development which has grown up is based upon state enabling legislation, but it is almost entirely a local system in all other important respects: comprehensive plans; zoning, building and housing codes; subdivision regulations; and others. There are also significant linkages between local planning and regulation of land use and tax support for all of the activities of local government.

States which pursue land use planning in order to deal with problems which are beyond the scope of local government or introduce consideration of factors of other than local concern or recognize relationships (such as that of land capability to land use) which are now generally ignored at the local level, find themselves in an ambivalent position: it appears to be logical and efficient to utilize a local system which is already in existence, even though this system may be the source of many of the problems which the state program must correct. Regardless of its objectives or procedures, States may encounter conflicts with their local governments wherever these governments are engaged in land use planning and regulation, and in many cases even where they are not.

Home Rule

Home rule is basically the right of a community to manage its own affairs. Unlike doctrines of legislative control, such as the special or general act system, a home rule municipality or county can, under a state constitution and laws, draft, adopt, amend, or revise a charter of its own government.

> The greatest amount of home rule that reasonably can be expected is that which would give to local government the fullest measure of self determination within the framework of American government. However, the idea has not been fully achieved even in the most advanced home rule jurisdiction. It is evident that an approach to home rule must be tempered by practical considerations.[28]

When mention is made of home rule States, the reference is to those States in which a specific delegation of home rule powers has been granted. These types of States must not be confused with those States where the laws pertaining to municipal corporations are quite liberal in permitting a broad scope of action by local governments and which are nearly equivalent to a grant of home rule. "Home rule as a definite and recognizable prerogative of local government may be granted either by the state constitution, the legislature, or by both."[29]

Substate Regionalism

America became an urban Nation during the first half of the twentieth century. In 1900, only a little over 30 million people of a total population of almost 76 million, or 39.7 percent, lived in places classified as urban by the Bureau of the Census. By mid-century the rural-urban distribution had reversed: 64 percent of the population, or almost 97 million people of a total population of more than 151 million, lived in urban communities. During this period, the Standard Metropolitan Statistical Areas delineated by the Bureau of the Census increased by 179 percent in population, or at a rate of 80 percent faster than the Nation as a whole.[30]

This imbalance in growth required utilization of large land areas surrounding older cities and was superimposed on a pattern of local government designed for rural conditions, frequently unincorporated and manned by part-time and unpaid officials. The traditional response of the cities during earlier periods of slower growth, to annex their fringe areas as they became urbanized, proved unworkable during this period since many cities were surrounded by other incorporated units which desired to preserve their own autonomy. In many States, annexation procedures were (and are) extremely cumbersome, sometimes requiring separate favorable votes by the residents of the unit annexing territory, the area to be annexed, and the remainder of the unit of which the area is part.

Substate regionalism has been the principal response to the inability of many local governments to cope with explosive urbanization and other problems which transcend their legal authority, financial ability, and territorial jurisdiction. This movement began in the larger metropolitan areas, where the problems of a complex urban community, bound together by common economic, social, cultural, and other interests, but divided into numerous political units, first emerged. It has since spread to other areas which also find the existing structure of local government an obstacle to effective action in rural concerns.

Planning for land use, transportation systems, and community facilities has become the focus of most regional efforts in the post-World War II period. Metropolitan planning agencies became eligible for federal funds through the 701 program in the Housing Act of 1954. The Federal-Aid Highway Act of 1962 provided that:

> after July 1, 1965, the Secretary [of Commerce, at that time] shall not approve . . . any program for projects in any urban area of more than fifty thousand population unless he finds that such projects are based on a continuing comprehensive transportation planning process carried on cooperatively by States and local communities.[31]

Since this process was defined by administrative regulation to include factors such as economic development, population, land use, zoning and other development regulations, open space, historic preservation, the environment, and aesthetics,[32] the planning activity required closely paralleled, or largely overlapped, the programs of many metropolitan planning agencies.

With a few widely scattered exceptions, substate regionalism has not produced a viable approach to land use planning. The areawide planning bodies are usually entirely advisory agencies, with no direct tie to any level of government which has executive or legislative functions. Neither local nor state governments have felt it necessary to follow, or even to receive, the advice of an amorphous group not responsible to them, and for which they are not directly responsible, and which has a territorial jurisdiction which does not coincide with that of any elected official.

Recognition of this problem has not led many regions or States to take what would appear to be the next logical step, creation of areawide governments, to carry out areawide plans.

The remedies which have been applied, such as designation of most regional planning agencies as areawide clearinghouses under OMB Circular A-95, do not really amount to empowering the agencies with power to implement their plans. The creation of councils of local governments has changed the actors in substate regionalism from appointed planning commissioners to elected local officials, and it has broadened regional interests to some extent. But these organizations have not shifted the power to implement plans from the local to the regional level, and they have not had any widespread or visible success in modifying the actions which local governments take toward greater conformance with areawide goals or plans.

These conflicts illustrate some of the more significant political realities of substate regionalism. Many regional bodies have been able to develop and apply technical resources on an areawide basis that would otherwise be unavailable to most local governments. They are, by and large, both more sensitive to local interests and better able to involve the public in the planning process than States have been in similar situations. But with only a very few exceptions, they have not been given the authority to implement their plans and they have not been successful in stimulating local governments to carry out their recommendations when a dispute between local and areawide interests arises. With the exception of federal grants and very limited state contributions, they remain dependent upon local governments for voluntary financial support, a situation which severely restricts their ability to even give independent advice.

If substate regionalism will not grow "from the bottom up," then its as yet unrealized potential may lie in action by the States. The States have the essential powers: to tax, to regulate through the police power, and to exercise eminent domain. The State has political accountability, and the Governor is in the best position to bring the major activities of state government in housing, transportation, pollution abatement, and other areas into conformance with regional plans. As state governments reassert themselves in land use, substate regionalism demands consideration as a possible mechanism for effectively structuring state-local relationships.

Recommendations, Findings, and Alternatives

Local Government

• *Role of Local Government.* Local governments and regional agencies should play a major role in implementing state land use programs, especially where they are already involved in land use planning and implementation through zoning, subdivision regulation, and other means. Procedures must be established to insure that local plans and actions are consistent with state policies and programs, that the appeals process does not permit or obscure subversion of the state program, and that the State can overrule local decisions which conflict with state programs.

• *State Assistance to Local Government.* States must provide substantial technical and financial support to localities operating a joint state-local land use program and must reserve the authority to operate the program in areas where local governments are unable or unwilling to do so.

• *Home Rule Considerations.* State land use activities should include adoption of legislation which establishes the relationship of the state program to local governments exercising home rule authority and which defines the conditions under which the state program will supersede local determinations. The conditions should include those of more than local interest or concern, those where a uniform approach is necessary, those where state action is essential due to an absence of local action, and others required by the type of approach the State adopts.

• *Reliance on Property Tax.* State land use programs should include or be coupled with actions which relieve land use decisions of their major local tax and revenue implications. As long as local governments must obtain most of their tax revenues from property taxes, land use decisions will continue to emphasize economic considerations over all other factors, including land capability. Major modifications in the current dependence of local government on property taxes, provisions for transfer of revenues among communities, and state financing of programs all play significant roles in effective land use programs.

• *Interlocal Conflict.* States should establish procedures for resolution of conflicts in land use plans, implementing measures, or other decisions which cross local governmental or regional boundaries. These can take the form of an appeals procedure and can be combined with mechanisms set up to hear and decide appeals from the application of state standards, criteria, or other requirements which are implemented through local governments and regional bodies or directly by a State. Adjudication of interlocal conflicts through this procedure should be mandatory before any court proceedings can be initiated.

• *Substate Regions.* A strong state role is essential to make substate regionalism work. This must go beyond passage of enabling legislation and division of a State into districts. The State must provide active technical and financial assistance in creating regional organizations for land use planning or any other purpose. It must clearly define the areawide and local responsibilities and prerogatives in ways which bring about effective and responsive mechanisms.

• *Review Authority.* Two options are available to States in establishing effective procedures for implementation of state land use programs through local governments and substate regional agencies: (1) to combine both planning and implementation at either the regional or the local level; or (2) to give areawide agencies authority to plan and to exercise an effective review over local implementing actions where these affect areawide concerns. In areas where home rule is well established, the second alternative may prove to be the more workable of the two. However, the latter alternative means that voluntary areawide planning agencies (e.g., councils of government) will require a state delegation of authority to make their review authority effective. Home rule members of such areawide agencies should not be able to veto areawide directives. The State should have ultimate responsibility for insuring local conformity and compliance with regional and statewide plans and policies.

State Government

• *Broad Involvement in the Management Process.* Mechanisms must be developed which permit those directly concerned and those who conduct closely related activities to participate in the development of land use policies and plans and management programs. These mechanisms should also assist in improving communication among agencies whose activities affect land use and in making their decisions and actions consistent with the land use program. A permanent committee structure working at the policy or advisory levels and including state, local, and federal representatives and the public should be established to facilitate participation, communication, and consistent action. The policy or advisory committee should be chaired by or report directly to the Governor, who should appoint state representatives and public members. Legislative members can be designated by statute or appointed by their respective houses. Representatives of local governments should be selected by the governments concerned, by an association of localities, by a regional body, or directly. Any federal representatives should be invited to participate by the Governor or by the committee itself. Arrangements should be made for coordination of land use programs with the related activities of any semijudicial regulatory agencies such as public utilities commissions and air and water quality control boards.

Multistate Regions

• *Interstate Cooperation.* States should create a new or utilize existing formal mechanisms to insure a coordinated and continuing response to land use issues which are interstate in scope. Informal arrangements will probably not be adequate over any extended period. Existing interstate organizations, new organizations, and creation of interstate compacts all offer ways in which the States can deal with interstate issues in land use planning and regulation. In designing a new instrument, or in modifying any of the existing types of organization, certain characteristics must be built in:

(a) The organization must be created through state initiative, not by federal mandate. This initiative can be in the form of a response to federal enabling legislation, but positive state interest and involvement from the inception of the operation is essential. A majority of the States in a multistate region should be able to establish an interstate organization without necessarily gaining the concurrence of every State within the area. This is necessary to prevent one State, unready or unwilling to address a regional issue, from hampering the others by its inaction.

(b) The State's representation in the organization must be from an appropriate level. For land use and most other programs, the Governor's participation is needed.

(c) State participation in the operation must include a continuing financial commitment.

(d) The purposes of the organization should explicitly extend to environmental, social, and economic concerns which have interstate aspects. The proliferation of multistate agencies, each addressing a different subject area, has already become a problem.

(e) Multistate organizations should delineate geographic areas for general jurisdiction and for major studies which incorporate entire States or major political subdivisions of States.

(f) These types of organizations must be structured so that, if there are federal participants, the state members can meet and act separately on matters of state concern, and jointly with the federal members on matters of mutual interest.

An organization with these characteristics can plan and coordinate land use and development while each State retains the authority to conduct management and regulatory activities in both interstate and intrastate situations. Alternatively, the multistate organization can be delegated specific or general operating or administrative functions if desired by the participating States. A principle which must be observed in selecting or designing an approach is that the State is the basic unit for management and regulation. A State can delegate its planning and coordinating responsibilities to an interstate body relatively easily, but the more substantive powers cannot be removed from the executive and legislative functions without excessive dilution.

Federal Government

• *Federal Role.* The federal role should recognize several factors:

(1) States are the primary authority for land use planning and regulation;

(2) Planning is a continuing process containing elements common to all States;

(3) The policies and regulations which emerge from this process must be effectively implemented and actions across areas which are divided by political jurisdiction or ownership must be consistent;

(4) The process of land use planning requires financial assistance, provision of essential information, and bringing federal actions which significantly affect land use into conformance with state and local land use programs whenever possible.

Any guidelines or administrative regulations which implement future federal land use policy or planning legislation must be universally applicable and have a normalizing effect on state programs. They must also have sufficient flexibility to accommodate the variations in the 50 States in their approach to land use planning and management. The intergovernmental relationships which have emerged among the States, through which land use policies and programs are implemented, are of particular concern and are subject to wide variations.

• *Planning for Federal Lands.* Long-range, comprehensive, and definitive land use plans should be prepared for all federally owned lands. States and local governments should play an effective role in formulating these plans, which should conform to state and local policies and plans for land use and development to the maximum extent consistent with national interests and federal agency missions and resources. It is especially important that private operations conducted on federal land under license or lease arrangements, and particularly those of a proprietary type, conform to state and local land use and development policies.

• *Use of Federal Lands.* States should secure their earliest possible involvement in the development of any procedures for designation of areas of particular land use concern by any federal agency or program, as well as in the actual designation of such areas.

• *Federal Program Coordination.* The A-95 review process should be strengthened by extending coverage to all federal programs which significantly influence land use, establishing a means of resolving serious conflicts between applicants and clearinghouses where land use is involved, and insuring that proposals which do affect land use are reviewed by the State's land use planning agency. All of these improvements can be accomplished by administrative action of the Office of Management and Budget.

3. Organization, Management, and Financing

Introduction*

The administrative aspects of land use planning and management activities were analyzed through nine case studies of States which have selected different overall approaches and which have reached different stages of the planning process. The States studied were Arizona, Arkansas, Colorado, Florida, Maine, Minnesota, Nebraska, Oregon, and Vermont. The case studies focused on four areas:

1. The history, context, and purpose of the program;
2. The organization and responsibilities of agencies conducting the program;
3. Integration or coordination of the program with other activities; and
4. Financing land use programs.

The Task Force considered the following specific questions to be of major importance in resolving key organization and management issues:

1. What problems precipitated state action?
2. What goals were set?
3. How was the program fitted into the governmental structure?
4. What interagency and intergovernmental relationships are necessary?
5. When and how do citizens participate in the process?
6. What are the functions of the State Legislature in the process?
7. How much does the program cost?
8. Where does the money come from?

Case Study Highlights

All of the States face serious problems as they organize or reorganize to conduct land use programs. The case studies illustrate the fact that the specific conditions vary from State to State and that the responses being developed reflect these differences.

Only in light of the relatively recent emergence of environmental concerns has the inherent authority of States in the area of land use control revealed its true significance. In the past, much of this authority had been delegated by the States to local governments who used it to enact zoning and subdivision regulations.

While this former delegation of authority does not prevent or preclude a State's ability to deal with the issues of land use, it may indicate lack of a ready-made structure at the state level wherein such activities could be located. As each State moves into this arena of land use legislation, it will have to decide the nature of the State's lead agency for implementation of that legislation.

In its consideration of this lead agency, the State must determine: (1) the responsibilities of that agency; (2) its location in the State's organizational framework; (3) its relationship to pertinent agencies that is conducive to

---

*For more detailed discussion, see Land Use Policy and Program Analysis Number 3, *Organization, Management, and Financing of State Land Use Programs* (Lexington, Kentucky: The Council of State Governments, November 1974).

coordination of all relevant functions, and (4) the anticipated costs of all land use related activities.

None of these considerations is entirely new to state governments which have over the past decade or two entered into a number of new activities at increasingly larger scales. Growth of local government assistance and transportation planning at the state level has helped States to develop a capacity for dealing with issues of physical development. Moreover, the introduction of — and the organizational changes to accommodate — environmental management and protection programs have helped prepare the States for their entrance into the related realm of land use planning, for their identification of relevant agencies to assist in this planning, and for their development of organizational schemes for the implementation of land use policies.

This is not to say that there exists a single, trouble-free process for States to follow in establishing their land use programs but, as the case studies demonstrate, each State can produce a workable mechanism for dealing with land use issues if only that State were to first take into account its own goals, objectives, capabilities, and structural limitations.

Dealing with the issues of organization, management, and finance on a broad basis multiplies the problems inherent in devising a structure and a method of carrying out any governmental function; but it is essential that organizational issues be addressed in comprehensive terms. This is particularly important if state land use programs are to be a unifying function for state actions in growth and development, rather than a planning activity operating in a narrow, compartmentalized manner.

Context and Objectives

The purposes and objectives of most state programs emphasize protection of natural resources, interposing state or areawide interests in matters which are clearly of greater than local concern, and balancing of economic development and environmental considerations. A few States incorporate the concept of a state general plan or a physical development or land use plan, but these are in the minority and one State, Colorado, has amended its legislation to delete this requirement.

Formulating the planning process and creating the institutions to conduct that process are generally considered most important.

A common thread runs through the rationale for those States initiating land use programs: a need to protect critical environmental areas such as wetlands, the need to deal with special development pressures from problem activities such as powerplants or second homes, actual or threatened loss of agricultural lands, and rapid population growth and urbanization. More specialized situations precipitated action in a few States: a water shortage in Florida, no local government organized to manage more than half of Maine's land area, and a logical extension of the movement to protect both the environment and the consumer in Oregon. Only two States, Arkansas and Nebraska, cite anticipated federal legislation as a reason for state involvement, and this was considered a secondary factor in both cases.

Most States emphasize a substantive rather than a procedural approach, identifying problems and formulating tentative policies and programs before selecting organizational mechanisms and instituting regulations.

Vermont provides the best example of the reverse procedure. The Vermont legislation first instituted a permit program for areas known to be susceptible to environmental damage and development exceeding a specified land area. Preparation of studies and plans were then scheduled over the following three years.

Strategies used to "raise the issue" also exhibit some similarity from State to State. The Florida program responded to a critical and immediate environmental problem, overdevelopment of the groundwater resources of south Florida. But most States are not experiencing such dramatic or widespread emergencies. The primary interest stemmed from private citizen organizations in Maine, Minnesota, and Oregon; from the Legislatures in Arizona, Colorado, and Nebraska; and from the Governors in Arkansas and Vermont. Public hearings and education programs, conferences, and official study groups were used in all three approaches. Idaho and Wyoming used extensive citizen surveys to determine attitudes and interests in state land use programs. Useful actions which can precede legislation include creation of study commissions and designation of responsible agencies through executive order, increasing financial resources through appropriations, drafting of legislation, land use surveys and analyses, and study of existing state laws influencing land use.

Lead Agency and Organizational Responsibilities

The predominant location for lead agency responsibilities is in the state planning office.

Only two States divide this function and in one the division is temporary. Most States also place the program under the Governor's direction. In Oregon, however, a Land Conservation and Development Commission (appointed by the Governor) supervises the program and appoints the director of their staff arm, the Department of Land Conservation and Development. All areas of critical concern must be designated by the Oregon Legislature. In all cases in which the state planning office is the lead agency, formulation of broader goals and policies is also involved. Most also administer the HUD planning assistance program and the federal grant review process established by Office of Management and Budget Circular A-95. Lead agencies frequently staff permanent regulatory commissions and temporary study groups.

The role of local governments and substate regional bodies is not yet clear in most of the States surveyed.

Florida, Oregon, and Vermont, however, all make extensive use of local governments or regional agencies. In Florida, local governments are required to adopt regulations for critical areas which are recommended by the State. If they

Figure 2
Lead Agencies

State	Agency
Arizona	State Planning and Office of Environmental Planning
Arkansas	State Planning
Colorado	Land Use Commission and State Planning
Florida	State Planning and the Administration Commission
Maine	State Planning (policy); Board of Environmental Protection (regulation)
Minnesota	State Planning
Nebraska	State Planning
Oregon	Land Conservation and Development Commission
Vermont	State Planning

fail to do so, the State can impose the regulations. Regional agencies in Florida review proposed developments of regional impact and report thereon to the local government concerned. Regional agencies and the State can also appeal local decisions on these proposals. In Vermont, District Environmental Commissions administer permits in accordance with the (interim) state plan. The Vermont Environmental Board may modify or reverse decisions of district commissions on appeal. Oregon places primary responsibility for land use planning at the local level by requiring that all counties and the city of Portland adopt comprehensive plans and implementing regulations based on state goals and planning guidelines.

State Legislatures

Legislatures have two key functions to perform in a state land use program. First, legislation establishing the program and its implementing procedures must be prepared, reviewed, and adopted. Second, the land use policies set forth in the legislation and the program for carrying out these policies must be continuously evaluated and revised when necessary as part of the continuing responsibility for legislative oversight. In two States, Colorado and Oregon, the Legislatures have set up joint committees on land use. One or two others use a select committee made up of the chairmen or other representatives of committees whose jurisdiction is related to land use. In most others the committees dealing with natural resources, environmental affairs, or state government have jurisdiction.

About half of the States studied used a formal committee to provide public involvement in developing the land use program.

In Arkansas, a 44-member advisory committee of citizens, legislators, and state and local officials held 12 public hearings and a statewide conference in preparing its report to the Governor. The eight District Environmental Commissions and the State Environmental Board in Vermont are comprised entirely of citizen members. Citizen task forces in each district assisted in preparing the land use plan, and copies of the plan were mailed to every household in the State.

Figure 3
Citizen Involvement Mechanisms

State	Mechanisms
Arizona	Environmental Planning Commission to hold hearings
Arkansas	Advisory Committee on Land Resource Management holding hearings
Colorado	Land Use Commission hearings
Florida	Administration Commission hearings on areas of critical state concern
	Division of State Planning preliminary hearings on critical areas and on regional impact process
	Regional planning agencies provide major public involvement
Maine	Eight substate districts for planning
Minnesota	Citizens' Commission on Minnesota's Future
Nebraska	N/A
Oregon	Land Conservation and Development Commission
Vermont	Formal hearings on plan

Program Coordination

Designation of the state planning agency as the lead agency for land use planning is the most frequently used device for coordinating functional planning. Maine has a cabinet subcommittee on land use, while Minnesota uses an Environmental Quality Council to administer related state legislation. This council can overrule decisions by state departments when it determines the environment is adversely affected. The state comprehensive plan is seen as the principal coordinating mechanism in Florida, while a modified program budgeting system is used in Arkansas.

Eight to 12 state agencies are typically involved in activities which are components of or closely related to land use programs.

Annual expenditures in those States surveyed ranged from $6 million to $9 million in 1973-74. Lead agency expenditures averaged approximately $1 million per year. Regional agencies and local governments also spent substantial amounts on land use planning and regulation, but these figures were not generally available. Most funds came from state appropriations. The HUD 701 program was the most important source of federal support.

Figure 4
Expenditures for State Land Use
Planning Programs

State	Fiscal year	Number of agencies	Expenditures (in millions)		
			State funds	Federal funds	Total
Arizona	1973	8	$5.0	$1.3	$6.3
Arkansas	1974	8	3.5	2.5	6.0
Colorado	1974	12	7.6	1.1	8.7
Florida	1974	1	1.4	0.1	1.5
Maine	1974	1	0.2	0.4	0.6
Minnesota	1973	1	0.4	N/A	N/A

The programs being developed or operated by the States surveyed reflect the fact that each State has its own laws, policies, and administrative structures which are designed to accomplish its goals and objectives. Any guidelines or administrative regulations which implement future federal land use policy or planning legislation must be universally applicable, but they must also have sufficient flexibility to accommodate the variations in the 50 States' approaches to land use planning and management. The intergovernmental relationships which have emerged among the States, through which land use policies and programs are implemented, are of particular concern.

Recommendations, Findings, and Alternatives

Context and Objectives of a State Land Use Management Program

• *The State as Trustee.* The purposes, goals, and policies for a state land use program must reflect the specific conditions in each State and be related to a conception of the State as the trustee of natural resources which must be managed so that they can be both used now by the citizens of the States and protected for the enjoyment of future citizens. This custodial role requires that the State consider environmental quality and economic development in more specific dimensions, perhaps including:

(a) Protecting valuable finite natural resources and areas which are exploitable;

(b) Relating the use of land to its natural and man-made characteristics;

(c) Reserving appropriate areas for economic development adequate to support the population;

(d) Relating the intensity of use of land to the type and level of public facilities and services available;

(e) Recognizing the areawide impacts of many development decisions;

(f) Achieving an appropriate balance of urban development, agricultural production, and other uses and non-uses of land; and

(g) Meeting major social needs which have significant land use relationships such as housing for all residents and supporting public institutions.

The State must also consider its responsibilities as a trustee of resources in light of the fact that decisions concerning the use of these resources are being made by the private sector and all levels of government as a continuous process usually without a framework by which the State can provide guidance, or even a consistent direction.

• *A Statement of Purposes.* A statement of goals and objectives should clarify the role that the State is anticipated to play in the land use planning process, define the kinds of problems in which the state or areawide interest is expected to transcend purely local concerns, and describe the mechanisms and intergovernmental relationships required for an effective joint state-local approach to these issues. The ways in which a state program can strengthen local efforts to cope with significant development issues should be identified. This is essential to counter an inaccurate and emotional portrayal of state land use programs as a takeover of local powers and prerogatives.

• *Why Get Involved?* A rigorous analysis of present or anticipated conditions in any State in terms of considerations such as those listed previously should disclose the basis for special action in that State; but, if a State cannot identify current or potential problems and needs in land management, it should not get involved. This implies that the question "Why get involved?" is more important and should precede the question of "How to get involved?" Until the "why" question can be answered, it is difficult to address the issues of procedures and mechanics intelligently. Certainly the decisions made in determining the purposes and goals of any program will also help to define the scope of that program, its place in the governmental structure, and its relations to other activities.

In considering the question, "Why did or should a State get involved in a land use program?," it seems that a State should not undertake this activity largely in response to prospective federal legislation on land use or closely related areas.

• *Sustaining Public Interest.* Initial public interest should be sustained throughout the continuing program, and it must adapt to the various stages of the planning process. Several of the case studies illustrate a logical progression of activities leading to a state land use program. Problems are identified by the public either through documentation of existing situations and their adverse potentials, or through a specific emergency such as the water shortage in southeastern Florida. This leads to organized citizen concern by existing environmental or other interest groups or by the formation of new groups directed to specific issues. This may be followed by a conference to further explore problems and possible responses, frequently called by the Governor. The next step may be appointment of an advisory committee by the Governor or creation of a study commission by the Legislature (or both) to develop more detailed information and formulate a program or draft legislation.

Informal meetings, formal hearings, and opinion polls can all be used as the goals and policies of the program are formulated and implementing procedures are designed. As these become operational, public involvement can be maintained through membership on the administering bodies, separate advisory or watchdog committees reporting to the Governor or Legislature, and general information programs. Public meetings and hearings can also be used in the evaluation of development proposals or permit applications as part of the operation of the program.

• *Developing the Issues.* Selection of strategies to identify and develop issues and actions which will lead to adoption of legislation must be geared to the specific conditions in each State, and particularly to the status of policy and functional planning programs in the natural resources and economic development fields. An educational program is an essential part of this strategy, as demonstrated in several States. These programs must be directed to the public, to local officials, and to legislators, since all of these must be aware of the existence of problems and accept the need for and feasibility of their solution before an effective program can be approved. This cannot be accomplished overnight, and probably not in a single legislative session. An intensive effort over a two- or three-year period should be anticipated. However, the tendency to extend this activity and overdebate the issues while serious problems grow worse can exhaust public and governmental interest. Simultaneous activities can include: establishing mechanisms for land use planning through executive orders and general reorganization statutes; strengthening policy and functional planning activities and improving their coordination through the budgetary process; documenting land use problems; demonstrating the value of a land use program as the core element for the functional planning and operations of the line agencies of state government, for local land use planning and regulations, and for private sector actions; and analyzing the capability of state and local governments and regional bodies to deal with development issues.

Lead Agency and Organizational Responsibilities

• *Basic Organizational Alternatives.* A state land use agency may be organized in one of four basic ways, with variations on each: (1) a departmental form, including a subdivision of a department; (2) a council or commission; (3) an authority with some degree of independence of other governmental operations; or (4) some type of interagency group. The location of this organization within the structure of government is virtually unconstrained.

• *Executive Responsibility v. Broad Representation.* The issue of executive responsibility v. broad participation is basic to the question of organizing a land use planning agency. The decisions which a State will make in responding to these issues depend on a vast array of factors which reflect the history and traditions of each State, the way it is organized to perform other functions, the size of this activity compared with other activities already a part of the structure, and many other, predominantly localized, concerns. But there are some common issues and problems which can at least be identified.

Many States are reorganizing to give their Governors more control through the appointive process. This is one way that a chief executive can be held responsible for the performance of the operating departments. Matters such as land use, coastal resources, or water quality also seem to require the participation of many diverse interests and specialists. These cannot be represented in a single department head. Often, these kinds of functions are assigned to a board, commission, or a council which ostensibly represents the more important interests concerned.

The members of these latter agencies are typically appointed for staggered terms which are longer than those of the elected official who appoints them, giving them some independence of the chief executive and of the political process, except for financing through the operating budget. The desire to build more and more diverse interests into the management process had led to more frequent use of councils and commissions for activities with much less pervasive scope than land use planning and management.

• *The Question of Home Rule.* Formulation of methods for local governments, special districts, and other units to participate in land use planning and management programs, while at the same time extending the decision-making process to include all of those affected by land use matters and introducing extralocal considerations, is among the most difficult organizational questions to resolve and should be evaluated in the unique context of each State. (See also Chapter 2.)

• *Organizing to Include the Public.* States should formulate procedures for meaningful public participation in areas such as land use policy, water quality management, and coastal zone regulation. As land use and natural resource management procedures become more technically sophisticated, and they must, many citizens will become more disenchanted with their ability to influence decisions. Most citizens will feel that they do not have adequate time to even find out and keep up with what is going on. In Vermont the chairmanship of an active District Environmental Commission is virtually a full-time job and other members spend an average of one day every two weeks at hearings. At the same time, legislative bodies, in many cases, are beginning to look askance at many public participation activities, feeling that their own role as representatives of the public is being undercut.

• *Organizational Criteria.* The following organizational criteria should be considered as each State evaluates alternative administrative approaches:

1. A unified approach to state land use policy and closely related natural resources and environmental programs is essential at the state level. This does not necessarily require that the entire activity be concentrated in a single organization, but basic policy direction, at a minimum, must be centralized. There are no techniques of coordination that will overcome the defects of complete functional decentralization when attempting to establish policy for the management of land and water resources. Program implementation responsibilities will probably be allocated among several agencies and levels of government.

2. The relationships between the planning, operating, and regulatory functions must be carefully considered and, in fact, a strong argument can be made for separating these activities, if adequate linkages are maintained. This position states that the planning component should be able to concentrate on policy issues unburdened by day-to-day operating problems. Operating agencies should be specialists, concentrating on carrying out the programs for which they are responsible, within a framework of established policies and plans. The regulatory agency should be free to enforce necessary regulations, unconstrained by prior involvement in their formulation or pride of parenthood in resource management programs. The alternative involves combining activities with dissimilar purposes, an approach which may increase efficiency but sacrifice a long-range and comprehensive viewpoint.

3. Placement of the land use planning and management functions in the

governmental structure must attempt to free this activity from institutional commitments or attitudinal bias to either the environmental or economic viewpoints and activities. Rationalizing the needs of these two is a continuous operation in the planning process; it cannot be done realistically or with credibility by an agency which has a preconceived orientation as a result of its place in the organizational framework.

4. The land use planning activity must be directly related to, and part of, general purpose government. Isolation, including isolation from the political process, will result in dilution of the effectiveness of the program in the long run.

5. Effective relationships between land use planning, capital investment programming, tax policy, and the functional planning activities which directly affect land use must be built into the structure. While the importance of different activities will vary from State to State and will change over time, water quality, transportation, recreation and conservation, and utility systems are typically the most significant.

• *Lead Agency Location.* The state planning agency appears to be a logical lead agency when the land use program is under the Governor's direction, or a logical source of staff support to a cabinet committee arrangement, if this agency is broadly involved in policy formulation and program evaluation. Where land use planning is undertaken by an agency with broad policy planning and management assistance responsibilities, functions such as the A-95 process and review of draft environmental impact statements should be combined with land use planning.

Program Coordination

• *Overview of the Problem.* Integration of a land use program with the many functions and interests which are closely related, and developing effective operating procedures in overlapping areas, must begin at the early stages of planning and not simply be a review of completed products. This is probably the most difficult aspect of the planning and management process. There are a number of programs where the need for coordination is particularly important. One of the most important for the coastal States will be coastal zone management. Recent federal legislation supporting state management programs will be of great importance to the 34 States and Territories eligible. The need to insure coordination between the coastal zone management program and the States' land use program is critical. The two efforts must be supportive of one another in all respects and in some cases it may be advisable to administer the coastal zone management program through the State's lead agency for land use. This approach can help insure program integration and can help maintain a needed statewide perspective in the management of the coastal zone.

Various environmental protection programs are in operation or are being developed which have direct land use implications. Statewide and areawide planning for water quality is one such program. Since water quality is in large part a function of the scale, type, and location of development, land use planning and controls become important elements in achieving and maintaining water quality standards.

The same can be said of air quality programs. Recent court decisions have made the land use control implications of air quality planning and enforcement even more apparent than they may have been in the past. Designation of areas where only minimum or no degradation of air quality will be allowed can profoundly affect development decisions. In most States, air and water quality planning and enforcement are not likely to be organizationally a part of the land use planning agency. This means that coordinative mechanisms must be found to insure compatibility. In general, air and water quality plans should fit into the state land use plan rather than vice versa. The state land use plan (or policies and guidelines) represents a more comprehensive statement of statewide needs. The type of close coordination required might best be achieved if the land use agency had a close organizational relationship to the Governor. It would also help if legislation specifically enumerated some of the key programs or agencies that must coordinate their actions with the land use agency.

There are any number of other state functions that must be coordinated with the land use planning process. Some are traditional and well entrenched, such as transportation planning; some are relatively new, such as housing finance; and others are highly technical, such as nuclear powerplant siting. Identifying the relevant functions that must be considered should be an initial land use agency task.

• *The Use of A-95.* If, as has been recommended, the land use program is made part of a more comprehensive, executive-level state planning office, the A-95 function can be used to insure that other plans and programs are consistent with the land use efforts. If the land use effort is not organizationally related to the A-95 clearinghouse, coordination becomes more difficult. One potential solution is to include specific language in legislation that sets out coordination responsibilities in an explicit and clearly stated manner.

• *Coordinating Federal, State, and Local Activities.* A State must develop the means to coordinate its own activities in ways that are consistent with and supportive of its land use goals and policies. This is an overriding concern in managing the land use program not only because it relates to program effectiveness, but because if the State cannot coordinate its own efforts, it will likely face considerable difficulty in its attempts to get local governments to coordinate their activities with the state effort. Local governments must become more effective in their own organization and management, not only under duress but under state leadership as well.

One method sometimes employed to help achieve coordination is to require another level of government to review all activities taking place within its borders for consistency. This is the approach generally employed by the federal government under its coastal zone management program. Each State is required to take the lead in assuring the compatibility of federal actions with the state program. It is the approach employed by Oregon in its land use program through county review of all relevant state and municipal plans and actions for consistency with state land use objectives. Requiring such review by another level of government can be an effective device to signal problems in coordination. However, it is not a substitute for effective intralevel coordination. The federal government should not expect the States to coordinate federal activities; the federal government must assume that primary responsibility. Likewise, regional or county review of state activities should not be a substitute for effective state interagency coordination.

Use of the state land use program as a coordinating mechanism which guides those state agencies and programs which have a major influence on land use is a desirable goal, but one which cannot be quickly achieved in many situations. Frequently, functional planning and regulatory activities will be well advanced, while land use planning is in the formative stage and will not be ready to move into implementation for two to five years. Sound environmental protection and facility planning programs cannot be held completely in abeyance until the land use program "catches up"; some decisions will have to be made and some action will have to be taken in many different areas in the interim. During this period, steps should be taken to insure that these are reviewed in terms of the land use program, to the extent that its stage of development permits.

• *Achieving Program Coordination.* Two general forms of organization can provide the necessary interrelationship to promote program coordination: (1) the land use planning agency established or designated with direct access, in a staff relationship, to the office of the Governor. The Governor is the only official in some States who can provide the degree of political leadership and public accountability needed and who has adequate authority over related activities of the executive branch; and (2) utilization of a cabinet committee or similar group of representatives of the state agencies which are most directly concerned with land use.

In either approach, the land use planning activity must be located in the decision-making and management chain, with access to closely related functions in the line agencies.

Financing

• *Cost.* Whatever its form, a state land use planning program will be an expensive process. The case studies do not support extensive generalization, but annual lead agency expenditures of perhaps $2 million to $3 million during program development and of similar amounts for operation of a management program are indicated, including assistance provided to local governments or regional bodies which participate in planning or implementation. Total expenditures for land use activities by all of the other agencies involved might run from four to six times this amount, but many of these expenditures are already being made and do not represent an additional financial burden.

• *Federal Support.* A well-formulated and effective program will require federal financial support in addition to state and local funds. Grants from a wide variety of federal programs should be used to support state land use planning and management efforts. Principal sources already available include funds appropriated under the Coastal Zone Management Act, the Clean Air Act of 1970, the Water Quality Act Amendments of 1972, Section 112 of the Federal-Aid Highway Act of 1973, and other programs. State management grants under Title V of the Public Works and Economic Development Act of 1965 may be available to States participating in a regional action planning commission. All of these can be used in conjunction with funds which may be made available in the future through federal land use planning legislation.

• *HUD 701.* If a federal land use planning assistance bill is passed, it should not be seen as a substitute for 701 funding. HUD 701 funds have been a necessary ingredient in most state land use planning programs. The HUD 701 program is especially useful in supplying support to local planning efforts and providing funds at the state level that serve to cement diverse programmatic efforts, promote coordination, and support special projects. Any initiatives to reduce 701 funding levels or to divert this program to other purposes must be viewed with utmost seriousness due to the great importance these funds have to the success of state land use planning efforts. This is particularly true since, unless and until federal land use planning legislation is passed and a grant program is funded, the 701 program provides the major federal support to most state land use activities.

• *Equity.* No level of government should require of another level that which the first is not able to financially support. This principle applies equally to the federal government and its possible requirements on the States, and to requirements the States might place on regional or local levels.

State Legislature

• *Role of State Legislature.* Legislatures must perform two key functions in a state land use program:

1. Legislation establishing the program and its implementing procedures must be prepared, reviewed, and adopted; and

2. The land use policies set forth in the legislation and the program for carrying out these policies must be continuously evaluated and revised as part of the continuing responsibility for legislative oversight.

• *Legislative Committee Structure.* As the Legislature performs its functions of establishing policy and overseeing its execution, relationships between the land use program and legislative operations should assume major importance. Land use planning and management will typically span the policy interests of many functional areas and thus the legislative committees and staffs which oversee them. The Legislatures in a few States have created committees which are comprised of representatives of the committees concerned with natural resources, transportation, and other related areas to meet these needs.

4. Critical Areas Programs

Introduction*

The concept of planning for and regulating areas of critical concern has emerged as a major element of the land use programs in most States which have undertaken this kind of activity. In some States, this concept forms the core of the entire program, while others use it as the leading edge of a broader effort because it emphasizes problems and needs which are clearly visible and well established in the minds of both the general public and state and local officials.

While the term "areas of critical concern" can be applied to a wide variety of physical, economic, and social conditions, the central and common characteristic is the existence of a problem which requires state or areawide attention. The Senate Committee on Interior and Insular Affairs has defined critical areas as:

> areas or uses which are of significant interest to or would have an impact upon inhabitants of an area far beyond the local jurisdiction which possesses the zoning or other land use regulatory powers.[33]

State programs often distinguish these as areas of critical state or regional concern, to identify them as being of more than purely local interest.

This terminology also causes some confusion with the term "critical environmental areas," which are areas designated or included in regulatory programs because of some existing natural characteristic of particular interest. Areas of critical concern can include these environmental areas as well as areas which are of interest for developmental or other reasons. This broader concept is used in this report.

The critical areas concept provides a means of demonstrating that the significance of some areas or facilities clearly extends beyond the boundaries of the communities in which they happen to be located.

These areas can be shown to require management at the areawide or state level in order to extend the decision-making process to all those who are really concerned or affected (see Figure 5). It also provides a means for States to recognize and implement their interests in land use and management of national resources which retains almost all local prerogatives intact and avoids building a centralized bureaucracy at the state or regional level while preventing duplication of the work of local planning and regulatory agencies. At the same time, defining, inventorying, designating, and regulating critical areas all place new demands on the States. An effective critical areas program will call upon technical, political, legal, financial, and organizational capabilities which are already frequently overburdened.

This state interest must be exercised without duplicating local actions at another level, without increasing the costs of land development unnecessarily, and without creating a time-consuming and inefficient procedure for making

---

*For more detailed discussion, see Land Use Policy and Program Analysis Number 4, *State of the Art for Designation of Areas of Critical Environmental Concern,* November 1974, and Number 5, *Issues and Recommendations — State Critical Areas Programs,* January 1975 (Lexington, Kentucky: The Council of State Governments).

land use decisions. The critical areas approach represents a method of focusing state interests and actions on problems which are beyond the abilities of local governments to deal with, while utilizing local agencies and procedures to the maximum extent possible.

As an example of such activity, the 1973 Florida Legislature passed an act that designated the Big Cypress Swamp as an area of critical state concern. This was an unusual legislative move because the Environmental Land and Water Management Act of 1972 (Act 380) provided a specific administrative procedure for designating an area of critical state concern. In the Big Cypress Conservation Act of 1973, the Legislature found that "the Big Cypress Area is an area containing and having a significant impact upon environmental and natural resources of regional and statewide importance."[34] The act:

> defined the area of critical state concern generally as the proposed Federal Preserve area "together with such contiguous land and water areas as are ecologically linked with the Everglades National Park, certain of the estuarine fisheries of south Florida, or the fresh water aquifer of south Florida." It exempted the Big Cypress from the acreage limit in Act 380 and bypassed the local governments in developing land regulations. Instead, the new law gave the division of state planning 120 days to recommend boundaries and regulations, and the governor and cabinet 45 days to adopt, modify, or reject the recommendations. The approved boundaries and regulations would take effect immediately, and be administered by local governments.[35]

The Final Report of the Division of State Planning included a recommendation that 859,000 acres be included in the area of critical state concern.

The bi-state area around Lake Tahoe provides another example. The lake was under development pressure and both Nevada and California agreed that the pristine qualities of the area should be preserved in a rational way. As a consequence, the Tahoe Regional Planning Compact of 1970 was created.

The resulting Tahoe Regional Planning Agency has prepared and adopted criteria for development in the area. The criteria are based on the capability of the land to support development. Development has not been denied, but it has been publicly directed.

Critical Areas Program Potentials

If the selection of critical areas is sufficiently broad to encompass the full range of state or regional concerns in land use and development, the critical areas approach can provide methods for both broadening and narrowing the resources planning and management process.

Both of these seemingly divergent objectives must be part of an effective state effort. First, States can use this approach to build new procedures into the planning process and to expand the basis for making decisions on when and how to use land. This is a major reorientation of long-established practice.

Figure 5

**Sample List of Critical Areas Identified
in State Programs and Legislation**

Agricultural land
Airports, approach zones, noise impact areas, and other surrounding areas
Areas above a stated altitude
Areas subject to frequent weather disasters
Coastlines, coastal areas, and tidewater
Communication facilities, transmission lines, and rights-of-way
Ecological communities, particularly those indicating characteristics of a physiographic province or biological phenomena or illustrating the process of succession and restoration, and rare or valuable ecosystems
Educational or research areas
Ethnic colonies
Flood hazard areas
Fossil evidence
Highway interchanges, particularly at the intersection of a limited access route with one which gives access to abutting properties
Historic sites, buildings, and district areas of a particular architectural style or quality, and archeological sites
Housing for low- or moderate-income groups or others who encounter problems in obtaining adequate shelter
Mass transit terminals or systems
Minerals extraction sites including inactive or mined areas
Natural areas which are unique or significant due to landform, vegetation, hydrologic features, flora, fauna, geologic formations, botanic interest, or zoological species or communities, whether terrestrial, ornithological, or aquatic
New communities, sites, and adjoining areas
Port facilities, deepwater anchorages, harbors, and channels
Powerplant sites and locations for other forms of energy production

Prime sites for economic development and job creation
Public facilities which support urban development such as water supply and sewerage systems and public schools
Recreation areas
Restricted population zones, such as in the vicinity of a nuclear powerplant or in an area of limited water supply
Rights-of-way and other means of access to water bodies
Rock outcrops and areas of very shallow soil cover
Scenic areas and vistas
Seismic or volcanic activity areas
Sites illustrating important scientific discoveries
Slopes which are too steep or otherwise unstable to support development or resist erosion
Soils which are unstable for construction or occupancy or unsuitable for on-site sewage disposal
Solid waste disposal areas
Storm protection facilities and natural features
Urban fringe areas, subject to rapid growth and development
Water supply sources: surface reservoirs, aquifers, and recharge areas
Wetlands — fresh and salt water, poorly drained areas, and areas of predominately sheet flow drainage
Wildlife habitat, particularly for endangered species, and seasonal havens.

More types of critical areas will be identified as additional States begin to utilize this approach.

Historically, land use planning and control has been largely concerned with land as an economic and cultural phenomenon. The prevailing view of land was that of economic, two-dimensional space. There was little concern for the features and processes of the natural environment which serve to differentiate one parcel of land from another. The plans and regulations were (and are) primarily based on its economic and social utility and were concerned with accommodating man-made structures and uses.

This limited approach to land use planning is no longer satisfactory. The natural characteristics of the land will have to be considered as much as its economic and social value. A new kind of land use planning is needed which goes beyond the task of allocating space for economic activities.[36]

Second, the critical areas approach makes it possible to limit state interest and action to matters which actually do have impacts which extend beyond the jurisdiction of one local government. The American Law Institute estimates that "at least 90 per cent of the land use decisions currently being made by local governments have no major effect on the state or national interest."[37] While the division of local and areawide interests should not be permitted to obscure the cumulative effect of a series of seemingly minor decisions, some kind of sorting procedure is obviously needed to permit States to concentrate on the relatively small proportion of matters where there is a legitimate nonlocal concern. The critical areas approach represents such a procedure.

Considerations

Designation of areas of critical concern through a state land use program is not simply a method of identifying areas where no growth should occur. The purpose of designation is to call attention to the importance of the area designated. In many cases it will be possible to permit development which is regulated so as to be "compatible with the basic environmental or renewable resources values or safety problems of the land in question." While it is true that "uncontrolled or incompatible development [would] result in significant damage to the environment, life or property, or the long-term public interest,"[38] it is equally true that some acceptable way to develop or use many such areas can be found; others must remain virtually unused or unoccupied if their values are to be preserved.

A key question in the critical areas approach is the relationship of state regulation of such areas to the adoption of an overall land use or development plan for the State. While a logical sequence of actions would seem to progress from preparation and adoption of a general plan covering an entire jurisdiction (a State or an established substate district) to regulation of land use or development in any part of that area, this process usually requires an extended time period, often of several years. Many problems will occur in the interim and, if no state action is taken, the chance to protect the area and to require that it be developed in accordance with its significant characteristics will be lost.

Finally, procedures must be devised which prevent the critical areas approach from becoming spot zoning at the state level. This requires a substantial understanding of the entire land resource and the demands placed upon it so that designation and regulation of critical areas will emphasize standards and information rather than intuition and political pressure. Achieving this kind of understanding without turning the planning process into a massive data collecting operation which becomes a substitute for decision-making requires that a clear distinction be made between a comprehensive perspective and complete and detailed information.

Critical Areas Selection

A systematic method of identifying areas of critical state concern is essential to insure that all important matters of more than local interest are included in the land use program. A logical procedure would involve (1) setting criteria for selection, (2) classifying broad types of areas, and (3) defining and identifying specific areas.

Criteria must be developed to meet the needs of different levels and types of governmental jurisdiction, for different geographic scales, and for different classes of resources. They can be extremely broad, with considerable potential ambiguity, or very explicit, concisely describing physical or biological phenomena. They will normally incorporate qualities such as functional significance, relative abundance, physical size, age, archetypal considerations, rarity or uniqueness, and endangered status.

Classification systems vary considerably in degree of specificity. Beyond those which can be derived directly from the criteria discussed above, two examples indicate the range available.

A study by the Smithsonian Institution notes that, at a minimum, a skeleton classification is needed to organize the resource classes which will be encountered in a survey of potential critical areas. Such a system might be limited to very general classes: physiographic, biological, and cultural categories would at least provide an initial screening.[39]

Federal land use legislation proposed in 1973-74 utilized much more specific classifications. Senate Bill 268 listed at least five classes of areas of critical state concern:

(1) Land sales or development projects [Sec. 202(d)];

(2) Areas of critical environmental concern [Sec. 203 (a-3-B)];

(3) Areas which are or may be impacted by key facilities [Sec. 203 (a-3-B)];

(4) The location of new communities and surrounding lands [Sec. 203 (a-3-D)]; and

(5) Large-scale development of more than local significance in its impact upon the environment [Sec. 203 (a-3-E)].

The bill, reported favorably by the House Committee on Interior and Insular Affairs, H.R. 10294, included only three of these: numbers 2, 3, and 5 above [Sec. 104 (b) and 105 (b, d, and 3)].

Once criteria, classifications, and types of critical areas have been established and validated, specific areas can be identified through an inventory process. There are a number of alternative procedures for making inventories available. One procedure would be a blanket inventory covering the entire State or region in terms of a detailed set of factors or variables, searching the area for land areas or other conditions that meet the criteria established for critical area designation. Another approach would be a sample area method involving a detailed study of a limited number of areas which have been identified through a more general screening process.

The inventory program, methods to be used, and mix of information types will reflect the criteria and classification system established for the critical areas program, but will also be influenced by the availability of data and the costs of collection. The quality and scope of resources information varies widely from State to State, and it is often scattered among several agencies and other sources. Data will probably be unavailable for some essential factors, or be so old that it is no longer valid.

Implementation

Three basic methods available to States for implementing state critical areas programs are:

(1) Direct planning and regulation by the States;

(2) Planning and regulation by local governments or by regional bodies in accordance with criteria and standards established by the State, and subject to state review and approval of local and regional implementing actions; and

(3) A combination of these two methods.

The most appropriate method will vary from one State to another, reflecting particular needs and established procedures. The general procedures for administering a critical areas program might include the following steps:

(1) Designation of specific areas, either by the State or by local governments or regional bodies acting in accordance with state criteria and standards. This action should have the effect of temporarily deferring development or changing the use of the area, except as permitted by the notice or other action designating the area.

(2) Formulation and adoption of regulations governing use and development of the area within a reasonable time following designation. This would presumably be done by the same agency making the designation. If the initial designation is by a local government or regional body, which then fails to adopt regulations, the State should do so under a backup authorization. If the State fails to do so, the designation should be cancelled automatically.

(3) Administration of the regulations through a permit program, including an appeals procedure, and other less coercive means of implementation.

In the period between the first and second steps, a landowner or developer has the opportunity to apply for a permit based on the controls and requirements set forth in the designation of the area and any controls in effect at the time of designation, with the most restrictive requirement applying in the case of a conflict. He also can seek judicial review if a permit is denied. It is advantageous to both the potential developer and the designating agency to minimize this period and to move into a permit operation based on adopted, permanent regulations as soon as possible.

Several methods of controlling the use and development of critical areas are available for administration of the critical areas program. These include conventional zoning and subdivision control techniques, performance standards geared to resource capabilities, land banking, property tax adjustments, transfer of development rights, and acquisition of land. Some of these are better suited to use at one level than another. Many local governments, for example, do not have the legal authority or financial resources to acquire land for this purpose, but they would be in a position to adjust property taxes (some already do so for other purposes such as to give tax relief to the elderly or veterans or to encourage industrial development or housing rehabilitation). New and largely untried concepts such as transfer of development rights and land banking could probably be done more effectively at the state level, where regional development considerations could be taken into account.

The regulatory methods selected by any State should reflect considerations of effective and efficient means of state involvement, appropriate jurisdictional levels for enactment and enforcement actions, political constraints, and competent ways of dealing with nonconforming uses and appeals procedures. A decision to acquire land or substantial interests in land, rather than implement some form of regulation in a critical area, introduces the additional constraint of funding availability and may blur the distinction between the fundamental powers of regulation under the police power and eminent domain. The latter issue is beyond the scope of this report and has been exhaustively analyzed elsewhere.[40] There is no doubt, however, that the States cannot afford to regulate all of their critical areas through acquisition of land or extensive compensation for loss of development rights.

Data Requirements

The methodology for gathering and interpreting data for designation and managing areas of critical state or areawide concern is still in its infancy.[41] Despite this stage of development the political viability of designating and regulating such an area will be highly dependent on this data. Without sufficient data to establish the environmental or other functions and importance of the area, it will be difficult to gain widespread acceptance of the designation.

In attempting to sustain the validity of designating and regulating critical areas, and particularly of areas of critical environmental concern, through litigation, the attorney will rely heavily on those who gathered and interpreted the initial data. These individuals should be able to explain: (1) the ecological, economic, or other functions of the area; (2) the relationship of the area to its surroundings; and (3) the effect of adverse development on the area.

When discussing the soundness and types of data necessary to sustain regulation of critical areas, it is essential that three points be considered: (1) the courts are factually oriented in their evaluation of land use controls, as applied to a particular parcel of land; (2) the courts will consider the purpose of the regulation; and (3) the courts will consider the impact of the regulation on the affected private property owner. These points in turn focus on three legal issues for which an adequate data base is essential.

First, the regulation must be specific and not vague: the landowner must know whether or not his property is subject to the regulation. This problem becomes more pronounced with certain types of critical areas regulation. Adding to this problem is the fact that many local units of government and local legislatures do not understand the need for specificity in designating a critical area. Their expertise lies more in the drawing of zoning boundaries along man-made features. When identifying critical areas such as wetlands and floodplains, the process becomes more complex since scientific and technical computations are often used to delineate the area. Once the area has been identified, the problem then arises that the area in question may cross property lines as well as natural features. In order to administer such an area it is necessary that fairly detailed maps be provided.

Second, the courts demand a higher degree of proof of the public need when the regulations in question impose severe economic burdens upon the private landowner. Therefore, it is advisable to determine in advance whether or not permissive or restrictive regulations will be adopted for the critical area. In making this advance determination, it will also be necessary to decide what type of data base is needed. Due to the fact that courts are hesitant to allow a restriction of all economic use of a person's property, much of the critical area regulation in existence allows for special permit uses. If special permit uses are authorized, it is necessary that data be available to evaluate a proposed use. The administrator must have information to determine what the probable effects of the proposed use will be if a permit is granted. In this instance it is evident that the data needed is of a very site specific nature.

The final issue deals with the methods of collecting data prior to the adoption of a regulatory program. Almost all critical area regulatory programs that have been instituted had very little regulatory-oriented data in the beginning. In order to overcome this problem three types of approaches have emerged. In the first method, a deadline for adoption of a management program or regulations for all areas of a given type is established which provides sufficient lead time to obtain the data needed. A second approach is to adopt regulations based on very rough initial delineations, and to refine these through the administrative process. A third technique is to shift the burden of data gathering to the developer as a prerequisite to a permit application. None of these procedures, however, should be considered a permanent substitute for systematic collection and analysis of the information needed in management programs.

Recommendations, Findings, and Alternatives

• *Component of Program.* The critical areas approach should be an integral part of the state land use program, regardless of the basic procedure used for implementing the program. It provides a method of insuring that many valid state interests are recognized for those States which essentially operate through local governments. It provides a means of adjusting the scale of the program to the varied conditions encountered by a State engaged in direct regulation. It is flexible enough to fit into any combination of these methods which a State develops to meet its specific needs.

• *State and Regional Interest.* All three of the methods suggested by the American Law Institute's draft Model Land Development Code should be used in identifying matters that will be of state or regional interest: areas which can be identified as critical because of their natural resources or the characteristics of land in either its original state or its present status of development; particular types of development which almost always become matters of more than local concern because of their environmental impacts or other aspects; and those types of development which can range from local to areawide or statewide impact depending on their size or scale.

• *Land Capability.* The critical areas approach should be used to help convert the land use planning process from one of simply allocating resources to meet demands to one of managing resources in accordance with their capabilities and characteristics. This requires that potential uses of critical areas be evaluated in terms of natural factors such as soil, topography, drainage, and climate, and cultural factors such as the type and level of public facilities and services available.

• *Regulation.* Critical area designations should be utilized to regulate the development of selected locations in accordance with their characteristics, whether positive or negative, and to aid in resolving conflicts between the needs of the economy and the limitations of the environment, rather than to express a no growth policy. Areas suitable for economic development which provide additional jobs for a growing labor force and areas which are more suitable for wildlife propagation or agriculture than for construction of buildings can both be included.

• *Identification Process.* Critical areas must be broadly defined in the initial stages of a state land use program to provide the flexibility demanded in a situation with many unknowns. State and regional interests cannot be fully anticipated in advance; many will emerge from the process of identifying and evaluating problem areas and activities. It will often be necessary to apply informed judgment to a limited data base in order to make initial determinations as to the different categories of areas and relative priority. These can be refined by more rigorous analysis as the quantity and quality of information available improves.

• *Designation.* Designation and regulation of critical areas should be authorized to precede the preparation and adoption of statewide studies and development plans for two of the three types of state or regional interests recommended above: those based on natural resources or land characteristics, and those based on particular types of development. State interest in the designation and regulation of areas based on the scale of development, however, cannot be adequately established outside of the broader planning framework. A site for a new community, for example, should not be designated except as part of a general development plan which provides the necessary information on the present and future locations and capacities of transportation facilities, water supply and sewage disposal systems, major recreation areas, and other essential elements of infrastructure; which deals with patterns and directions of urbanization; and which evaluates areas which might be potential sites for new communities in terms of maintenance of their present uses and conversion to a variety of alternative uses. The critical areas procedure should not be used to avoid the other considerations that preparation and adoption of such a plan entail.

• *Context.* Both to support the designation and regulation of critical areas more fully, and to prevent transfer of the worst of current local zoning practices to the state or regional level. The critical areas approach should be an integral part of a broader state land use program. At a minimum, this program should include appraisal of physical conditions throughout the State and evaluation of the social and economic demands which will be placed on these resources.

• *Criteria for Selection.* The criteria for identifying areas of critical concern to a State or region should combine resource management objectives and factors which will be useful in formulating classifications for screening and selecting areas. The classification system need be no more detailed than is necessary to organize and direct the screening and selection process. A general system of categories, each incorporating a number of types of critical areas, is potentially more useful than are restrictive, detailed classifications, particularly in the early stages of a state critical areas program. A skeleton system can always be refined and subdivided as the program proceeds.

• *Reasonableness.* A complete process of setting criteria for identifying matters which are of state interest, classifying broad types of areas for screening and selecting areas, and defining specific areas and levels of state concern, is essential to keeping a critical areas program within reasonable bounds. Without the discipline that this process imposes, the geographic scope and subject matter involved can easily expand to the point at which the program becomes unmanageable and ineffective.

• *Sample Inventory.* Most States will find some kind of sample area inventory procedure most feasible for use in critical areas programs in terms of availability of data and staff and financial limitations. Use of this method requires more careful consideration of the criteria used to select areas in order to reduce the chance of a category being overlooked completely.

• *Documentation.* Systematic documentation of the designation of critical areas, incorporating all of the information used in making the designation, is essential to support a regulatory program and to justify the designation and control of the area in any litigation. Use of a standard format for designation will help insure that this requirement is met. This should not be interpreted as requiring that designation of an area as critical be delayed until all of the possible information about it is obtained, but that all information which is available about an area be assembled or recorded and be used in the designation process.

- *Local Administration.* Major consideration should be given to use of local governments or regional bodies in the administration of critical areas programs. A workable method is to have all decisions that can be made in accordance with adopted state standards or regulations, made at the local level. The appeals process would be conducted by, or closely monitored by, the State. However, any use of local governments in program implementation makes it necessary that the State prescribe uniform and detailed regulations for program administration, including creation and maintenance of complete records of actions taken on each permit application, the specific findings made, and the reasons therefor. This is essential to insure that a complete record is available for state review of implementing actions for conformance with critical areas objectives and regulations and for any litigation. The type of record-keeping which characterizes many local land use and development regulatory activities and appeals procedures is not adequate for these purposes.

- *Performance Standards.* A combination of performance standards based on analysis of the capability of resources to support development and conventional zoning techniques appears to offer the best method of regulating most types of critical areas. Whatever the method, regulations should be as explicit as possible so that both the landowner and the administering agency can determine what development or use is or is not acceptable, with a minimum of interpretation.

- *Litigation.* When litigation occurs, the administering agencies must develop and present a complete and detailed factual basis for the designation of an area, the specific regulations used, and the adverse impacts of the development or use proposed, in order to obtain a decision that goes as far as possible toward accomplishing the objectives of the critical areas program. Two factors are of primary importance in responding to a court challenge to the designation or regulation of a critical area. First, the presentation of the designation process, the reasons for a specific designation, and the necessity of the use or development regulations applied must be factually documented. The "Brandeis brief" is particularly relevant in this kind of proceeding. Second, expert witnesses must be used who can determine and describe: the conditions existing in the critical area; the level or type of activity which the resource can support; and the adverse results of exceeding these limits, to the extent that these can be established through scientific evidence, assumptions, and evaluations made by those qualified to do so by education and experience in the disciplines concerned.

5. Public Involvement

Introduction*

Citizen participation in state land use planning programs is a dynamic and incremental process of furthering involvement in the planning process on the part of all citizens, and particularly those citizens who have traditionally been unwilling or unable to be involved. This includes citizen education, a process wherein the layman is supplied with a wide range of information (representative of several points of view) which will enhance the quality of citizen input to the state land use planning process.

Efforts to involve the public in this process must stem from an attitude on the part of the agencies conducting these activities that they are accessible to the public and responsive to their opinions as a matter of course. Officials and technicians must recognize a widespread lack of public confidence in the way government and its agencies are handling public affairs. Many citizens are angered and frustrated because they feel totally excluded from the mainstream of government decisions made without adequate public information, comment, or participation. Conflicting demands and intense economic pressures on the uses of the Nation's land resources place even greater requirements on politicians and decision-makers. Too many land use judgments have been single-purpose and economically motivated and have often overlooked or neglected complementary social and environmental needs of the community. However,

> the reason citizen participation must be pursued is that it is a basic and inalienable right of the American people. There is no question . . . whether there should be maximum participation or not, or even what its effect will be or has been. Rather, the concern must be to establish the institutional mechanisms which will most successfully guarantee the right of participation to all citizens.[42]

Effective public participation in a land use planning and management program, or in any other activity, must reflect some essential characteristics. The public must be *interested* in the process and its results if they are to invest the time necessary to make their participation meaningful. To help develop and sustain interest is an integral part of a public involvement effort. The public which participates must be *representative*. That is, all segments of the population must participate, preferably in numbers proportionate to their presence in the total population. Third, the participants must be *informed*. Information and educational programs are an important part (but only part) of public involvement. Fourth, *responsible* participation should be sought by officials and technicians and given by the public. This means that the public must be involved in the important aspects of the issue under consideration in a way that accepts intelligent questions and suggestions and avoids both deception and demagoguery. Finally, the involvement of the public must be *timely;* opinions must be obtained and considered before decisions are made.

---

*For more detailed discussion, see Land Use Policy and Program Analysis Number 6, *Manpower Needs for State Land Use Planning and Public Involvement in State Land Use Planning* (Lexington, Kentucky: The Council of State Governments, 1975).

Objectives

A public involvement effort which embodies these characteristics can address several of the following objectives with some success.

(a) Problems and goals are identified and often some degree of agreement on a course of action is achieved through widespread discussions.

(b) Information and feedback occur. To develop viable solutions and conduct realistic plan evaluations, it is necessary to open avenues for direct communication between government officials and the public. The program should assist officials in identifying local interests and in understanding perceptions of problems and needs. Public assessments of appropriate institutional arrangements should be sought, as well as public reactions to and preferences for alternatives.

(c) Trust in the land use planning process is fostered. The program should be characterized by frank and open interaction among officials and the public.

The methods of bringing about meaningful public participation are not well developed. Some basics, however, can be identified. It is often necessary to institutionalize the process by forming committees, councils, or other formal organizations. This helps to sustain interest over an extended period, but runs the risk of limiting participation to an unrepresentative (or preselected) public. It also is usually more workable to structure approaches to public involvement through regularly scheduled meetings, newsletters, and other devices. Again, this runs the risk of increasing participation by a limited number at the expense of broad representation. Communication between public officials and agencies and the public, in both directions, is an obvious essential. An attempt to involve the public while withholding any significant information will usually result in disaster. Public involvement carries with it a responsibility incumbent on the agency for full and understandable disclosure.

Funding of the effort is equally essential — public involvement cannot be treated as a no-cost or even as a low-budget aspect of a larger program. *Perhaps most important to long-term credibility is that all comments, suggestions, and questions which are not patently frivolous must be responded to and the response must reach the public which is participating.*

A number of more specific procedural and structural mechanisms can be used within the guidelines outlined above. The following methods have all been employed by state land use programs:

(a) Citizen study groups and task forces — these can be used before and during the planning process to surface various issues that are of concern to the citizens of the State.

(b) Formal public hearings and meetings — these are often required by statute, and they provide a forum for expression of both organized and individual interests. However, input at such proceedings is often more of a reactive rather than a creative nature.

(c) Ad hoc and advisory committees — these two mechanisms are most effective when they have been specifically designed to be broadly representative of geographic areas and of interests relating to land uses and land use decisions. Their effectiveness is also increased when they have concrete responsibilities and sufficient resources to accomplish them.

(d) Questionnaire surveys — this method can be most useful in surfacing attitudes, priorities, and perceptions. Great care must be exercised with this method to insure that the survey measures what it is intended to measure. The survey method can be expensive, but it can also produce helpful input.

(e) Surveys made by citizens — the benefit of using this method is that the interviewer gets the opportunity to determine what his fellow citizens' reactions are to the concept of state land use planning, or has an opportunity to participate in collection of data which is used later to formulate alternative plans and make land use decisions. It can also be less costly than survey interviews conducted by paid interviewers.

(f) Public membership on policy or advisory boards — these can be comprised of both official and public members, or restricted to public members only. The activities of these groups normally span the entire planning process from problem definition and goal setting to adoption of management mechanisms. Most of the other methods available are more useful at a particular point or points in the process.

(g) The citizen jury — this is an adaptation of the method above in which a representative group of citizens is officially convened to evaluate a program by overseeing the entire process and evaluating the recommendations or actions which result.

(h) Elementary, high school, junior college and university programs — these programs are formal, although not necessarily separately identified, efforts which should involve both education and participation. These are most successful when integrated into all appropriate aspects of the regular curriculum rather than being conducted as separate classes or activities which are isolated from related subjects. Teacher preparation through formal training is essential.

Recommendations, Findings, and Alternatives

• *Scope.* Development of methods by which the lead state agency can inform and educate the general public should be given major consideration.

• *Program Design.* A public involvement program that will be acceptable to the lay citizen should incorporate the following features:

(a) The state officials who are responsible for the state land use planning process should be readily accessible to the general public;

(b) The state official in charge of the land use program should be as responsive to the needs and preferences of the citizens as is possible; and

(c) The program must be designed to insure a degree of accountability for all decisions made that affect the general public.

• *Program Objectives.* A public involvement program should be directed to specific objectives, such as:

(a) To overcome lack of, or problems of, established political mechanisms so as to reach segments of the population not adequately represented in the planning and decision-making process;

(b) To communicate the concerns of interested citizens;

(c) To build public confidence in the land use planning process;

(d) To inform the public of plans, policies, regulations, and problems;

(e) To reflect changes in public perception of their area, its needs and resources, and how best to use resources;

(f) To improve compliance with the eventual program; and

(g) To disseminate and make readily available information that can lead to better land use decisions.

• *Techniques.* Public involvement should be established on a continuing basis throughout the entire program. Appropriate techniques of involvement should be used at each stage of the planning process. The following examples of involvement indicate the broad areas to be considered in the planning process.

Identify Needs. Study groups, task forces, informal meetings, and use of questionnaire surveys are all methods that can be used to identify problems. In addition, many citizen organizations have studies already available that can help identify the problems.

Inventory Resources. Many of the methods above can be used but, in addition, citizen group surveys or surveys conducted by students in elementary and secondary schools, junior colleges, and universities can be a way to motivate people to think about land use resources.

Analysis of Information. Discussion of information about and analysis of problems and resources and their relation to wise planning for the land can take place in informal meetings, public hearings, workshops, and conferences.

Plan Formulation and Implementation. In arriving at land use planning goals and devising mechanisms for implementation, informal meetings, public hearings, and advisory committees are useful. Other techniques, such as simulation models and gaming, deserve attention. Citizen juries appointed to literally judge plans might also be used.

Monitoring and Enforcement. These two functions are crucial. Too often citizens relax once a law has passed and they do not see how important enforcement is. Enforcement comes about only through efficient monitoring of results. This requires a sustained effort and continued commitment to the goals of a program. These functions are best performed by advisory committees and policy boards with public membership and through public hearings.

Evaluation. Any land use program will need to be evaluated periodically as to its effectiveness. It should also be modified to reflect changing conditions in the State. Seminars, conferences, and public hearings are all good vehicles for the evaluation process. Questionnaire and telephone surveys are also useful. Some state agencies are using public television with call-in facilities to sound out public opinion.

• *Staffing.* Staff to carry out the public involvement program and to provide official-public liaison should be designated. Staff should either be specifically assigned or allocated specified time periods for this function by state agencies.

- *Funding.* Public involvement must be adequately funded. It is not a low- or no-cost item in a land use planning program budget. The funding level must be consistently high enough to insure continued citizen input. Special participation projects such as surveys, conferences, and community workshops will require funding over and above the continuing level.
- *Media.* A public information and involvement program should make maximum use of the media. Preparation of information by state agencies for use by the media assures that the public is getting the information it needs to keep abreast of land use problems, programs, and opportunities. This is a crucial part of the program since effective participation depends on an informed public. Agencies can also prepare or have prepared slide shows, films, and other visual materials for use by the media, so that information can be carried to a wider audience through the press and audio-visual media. Questionnaires that are completed at the end of the showing of a film or slide show are an extremely effective way to present land use issues and alternatives to be considered by the general public. While official notice of public hearings in the newspaper serves a purpose, it does not substitute for a well-rounded media informational program.

6. Manpower Needs

Introduction*

A survey of the States as of September 1974 showed that 21 of the 50 States were involved in some kind of land use planning program at that time, and that eight of these included a regulatory function;[43] other States have land use bills under consideration or programs in preparation. All of this activity has occurred without federal land use legislation. As noted previously, these States are approaching land use and natural resources management through several different methods. Most are concerned with the identification of critical areas and developments of areawide impact, but the particular types of areas and activities included in the management program vary greatly from State to State. Other States are emphasizing a comprehensive approach to management on a statewide basis, or are concentrating on those areas where local governments are not engaged in management programs or where no local governments have been organized.

All of these alternatives embody a major shift in land use planning and regulation as it has been practiced, particularly at the local level, from simply allocating resources in an attempt to meet virtually unconstrained demands to management of resources in accordance with their characteristics and capabilities. This requires that the agencies conducting land use programs employ new talents and skills.

State land use programs also place new demands on local governments and regional planning bodies, since most States will utilize these levels in both planning and management operations. In addition to their present activities in comprehensive and land use planning and implementation through zoning, subdivision regulations, official maps, capital budgets, and other mechanisms, many local and regional agencies will be required to observe and administer state goals, standards, and criteria.

Personnel Requirements

The growing state involvement in land use and natural resources programs and their expansion from regulation to broader management concerns will result in an increase in the number of persons required to administer land use programs, and a significant expansion of the types of knowledge and experience required at all levels. This broadening of the interdisciplinary approach which has always characterized land use planning creates substantial new manpower requirements.

The numbers and kinds of personnel needed to conduct state land use programs are determined by factors such as:

(1) The State's general approach to management of land and related resources (see "Major Issues" in Chapter 1).

(2) The specific content of the program. A program which gives heavy emphasis to preservation of agricultural lands, for example, has different staff

---

*For more detailed discussion, see Land Use Policy and Program Analysis Number 6, *Manpower Needs for State Land Use Planning and Public Involvements in State Land Use Planning* (Lexington, Kentucky: The Council of State Governments, 1975).

needs than has one directed to protection of wetlands.

(3) Assistance provided by other agencies with expertise in particular areas of concern.

(4) The time frame established for the program and the sequence of actions to be taken. Immediate initiation of regulatory activities requires a different staff mix than initiation of these activities at a later stage in the planning process. The length of time available to conduct the process largely determines the size of staff required.

(5) The geographic area and complexity of the situation to be covered by the program also help determine staff size and composition.

The operating experience available indicates that the techniques which the States are developing to manage land and related natural resources will require large amounts of staff time. Florida estimates that it took about 3,500 hours of staff time to work up the Big Cypress Swamp Critical Area, including assembling and evaluating data and preparing a recommendation, but not including the implementing process or public involvement. In Florida, the five professionals in the critical area section could only handle two critical areas. In all, 25 professionals in the division of state planning were involved in the land planning and management program in one year; 26 more positions were being requested. The total budget for the land use program in 1973 came to about $1.5 million, including $450,000 for regional planning agencies. The state planning director estimated that it would take $3.5 million annually to fully implement the law.[44]

Reliable information on the availability of people trained in the many disciplines which must contribute to the state land use planning process is not available. Obviously, most States will encounter serious problems in assembling staffs which are representative of even a few of the fields and specialities which are essential to a comprehensive program; desirably these would include persons with training and experience in physical and social planning, the natural and earth sciences, the behavioral sciences, econometricians, attorneys, computer programmers and data storage and manipulation people, designers capable of working at a variety of scales from the project to the regional levels, simulation experts, and specialists in communication through multimedia techniques.[45] *It will be even more difficult to introduce those with particular training at the points in the process at which they are most needed. Limited financial resources will further complicate the manpower availability situation.*

These problems will require most States to rely heavily on staff members trained in planning and closely related fields, supplemented by other specialists on the staff and in other governmental agencies and universities.

While state manpower needs for land use programs cannot be met simply by training more planners, recent trends in this field provide some indicators of the general problem. The American Society of Planning Officials conducts an annual survey of planning education which provides data on the availability of persons trained in planning. Although the ASPO survey shows that the total number of students enrolled in planning schools has increased from 586 in 1958 to 4,982 in 1973, there has been a very definite leveling off in the number of students enrolled in planning programs in recent years. This has happened even though the number of schools offering programs has doubled since 1964. Since 1970, about 1,100 planning degrees have been granted annually at all levels, and this figure too appears to be leveling (discounting the time lag for those enrolled in prior years of high enrollment).[46] Similar situations will be encountered in all the other disciplines which must be involved in the land planning process.

Recommendations, Findings, and Alternatives

• *Continuing Education.* Continuing education programs for professional planners and personnel from allied professions involved in planning activity should be utilized. The Florida Division of State Planning, for example, is running an educational program in connection with the administration and handling of developments of regional impact. Personnel departments at all levels of government and colleges and universities can also conduct in-service and other training programs for persons in the field. Land grant universities have long experience in continuing education which should be utilized to help meet this need.

• *Retraining.* Retraining programs to familiarize staff members with new requirements and procedures and update or replace obsolete skills should be conducted. Land use programs may require agencies to redirect their efforts and reallocate staff resources. Persons experienced in the planning process but with professional or technical education and experience in other respects of planning should be given opportunities to acquire the training needed to perform in land use programs. All staff members, regardless of present level, recent assignments, or general background, should have opportunities to keep pace with this rapidly changing field through formal and informal training.

• *Personnel Sharing.* Formal or informal arrangements for the participation of specialists employed by the line departments and other agencies of state government should be entered into in the planning program. Procedures such as those established by the Intergovernmental Personnel Act to facilitate movement of staff between levels of government should be used. Many of the "Action Plans" prepared by States for highway planning purposes in response to requirements of the U.S. Department of Transportation[47] contain such arrangements and involve the same subject areas that are of concern in land use planning. Personnel policies should be flexible enough to permit and encourage people to move between levels of government and between agencies at the same level. This can make specialists available to a number of programs requiring input from a given field, improve interagency and intergovernmental coordination and understanding of missions and procedures, and make the individuals concerned more versatile and more valuable.

• *Para-professionals.* Use should be made of para-professionals to perform such time-consuming tasks as drafting, statistical activity, survey and interview work, etc. Underutilization of professional staff members is a common problem of public agencies and a major factor in employee dissatisfaction and agency inefficiency. Adequate staffing of the essential but less complex phases of the program will free professionally qualified people for tasks better suited to their skills and salary, and will improve productivity.

• *Higher Education.* Resources available through public and private colleges and universities should be utilized. Instructional departments and research institutes will often have ready access to persons with many of the skills which are needed in the management program. Minnesota and New York have used this method to build a land resource data base. Other States have drawn on university resources as part of their coastal zone management programs. The current lack of financial support for academic research at levels comparable to those of the past can be replaced in part by involvement of faculty and students in land use programs.

• *Consultants.* Professional consulting services should be utilized when necessary to supplement staff resources by providing skills not otherwise available or by increasing the manpower available so as to shorten the time required for a given activity. Consultants can provide many of the skills needed to identify problems, analyze alternative courses of action, and prepare management programs. However, continuing reliance on consulting services in administering the program is not desirable since it fails to establish a continuing capacity.

• *Intergovernmental Teams.* Some of the needs for specialized personnel at the local level can be met by organizing teams at the state and regional levels who can provide such assistance on a consulting basis. Individuals or teams can be made available to local governments and substate regional bodies to augment existing staffs. This approach can be used to meet the needs of smaller agencies which lack basic planning expertise and to provide special skills which are needed for a limited period or to attack a specific problem. These "circuit riders" can operate on either a statewide or a substitute regional basis. Multistate agencies could also offer assistance in extremely specialized areas.

• *Environmental Awareness Centers.* In the long run, land use planning and management agencies cannot hope to maintain staffs which are adequate in either numbers or diversity to meet all needs. Approaches such as an "Environmental Awareness Center" in each state capitol, proposed by Professor Philip H. Lewis, Jr., should be considered. These centers would serve as

> informational (nerve) centers, simulation labs, environmental gaming centers, integrated environmental museums; centers that continually present clear pictures and concepts about people and their environment, the problems, potentials and casual relationships.[48]

The centers would provide a functional link between state governments and the universities, corporations, interest groups, and the general public. A series of "process teams" would be organized around both permanent and "loaned" staff as a flexible means of providing the breadth of talent necessary to conduct the management process. The process teams are interdisciplinary planning groups and would include teams with the following specialties: natural and earth sciences, behavioral science; environmetrics, design, implementation, simulation, and communications.

7. Data Needs and Resources

Introduction*

The collection of data represents both an essential activity and a source of major problems in land use planning. Land use planning at any level requires a wide range of information. Population numbers, densities, and characteristics, economic activities and employment levels, environmental and social conditions, natural resources and their capabilities and limitations, transportation, housing, utility systems, and public services and facilities are some of the areas in which information on current status, past trends, and possible future directions is essential. Both the quantitative and the qualitative dimensions of these factors must be described.

States face massive problems in creating a data base which is adequate for land use planning at the state level, and which will support essential corollary activities at the interstate, substate regional, and local levels. These are not primarily problems of the availability of information. A recent study notes that:

> As astounding acceleration in the accumulation of basic or raw data has occurred in recent decades . . . a many-faceted technological explosion has made it possible to obtain, process, and disseminate a greater variety of information more expeditiously and efficiently.[49]

Nevertheless, "the needs of the planning practitioner and the researcher are not being met" because data is not managed and organized within systems which are useful to the technician, the decision-maker, or the public. "The data are coming because the facility is there and not as the result of identified need. What is required is a concerted effort to close the gap between the data being generated and the specific needs of the practitioner,"[50] and to eliminate data collection and storage activities which are not serving any identifiable purpose.

The introduction of concepts such as the carrying capacity of land and limitation of the use of land to levels permitted by the natural and man-made characteristics of resources, multiplies data problems. Critical areas programs further extend the scope of data needs, from very general assessment of growth patterns and resource capabilities to detailed evaluation of biological, topographic, and other conditions.

State Data Systems

Some data storage systems have been constructed that are so complex, extensive, and detailed that they represent a major obstacle to both updating and using information. Many past efforts in this field have devoted much of their resources to data collection operations and yet have been unable to produce information when it was needed to evaluate alternative courses of action or make a decision. The potential of these problems to delay, disrupt, and exhaust the

---

*For more detailed discussion, see Land Use Policy and Program Analysis Number 2, *Data Needs and Resources for State Land Use Planning* (Lexington, Kentucky: The Council of State Governments, September 1974).

resources of state land use planning programs is magnified by the scale of these operations.

The data requirements of state land use planning programs can only be kept within realistic limits by determining the data needs of state programs in terms of the scope and content of the activities to be undertaken. The determination of data requirements is a reasonably straightforward technical question once this distribution of activities is known. Identifying this distribution of activities among governmental levels and among agencies at any level represents a significant task in itself, and one which cannot be overlooked in the state land use planning process.

States will encounter a circular relationship in establishing goals and policies for the development and use of land. Data will be needed to formulate and evaluate policy alternatives and to select courses of action. Programs designed to achieve the resulting objectives will in turn have their own data requirements, many of which will overlap or be similar to those of policy formulation. In addition, the data collection can best be performed if it is done within the context of the policies to be formulated.

This suggests that data collection and storage activities must be structured in an open-ended manner and must be undertaken incrementally in order to meet the needs of all phases of the planning process and still remain in scale with other activities as they progress.

No comprehensive appraisal has been made of the capability of States to assemble the data required for land use planning and management programs. However, a preliminary evaluation has been made, as of September 1973, using four indicators:

(1) The presence or absence of a statewide land use map (regardless of age);

(2) The current use of land use data in state planning activities;

(3) Recent acquisition and analysis of land use data; and

(4) Technical capability in remote sensing and land use data analysis.

These criteria indicate that less than two fifths of the States probably have significant ability to generate land use information.[51] Capabilities in gathering other essential information vary, with most States having reasonably good access to population data. However, more serious difficulties are encountered in obtaining economic and natural resources data.

Federal support to the States in meeting their data needs is essential. This assistance could be provided through national land use legislation such as that considered by Congress during 1973-74, or through other legislation. A substantial amount of support could also be made available, without further legislation, by better organization of existing federal data collection and dissemination activities.

All data collection and storage activities must be operated on the principle that data needs, in terms of type, quantity, geographic organization, accuracy, and all other important dimensions, cannot be determined in a vacuum. The manpower, technical, and financial resources available will never permit us to find out all that we would really like to know. Data needs for state land use planning must be determined by the issues which the planning process will address, the planning concepts and approaches embodied in the process, and the methods that will be used to implement land and resources management programs. If state land use programs are to have an impact on decisions about the way land and resources are used, data collection, processing, and storage activities must be an integral part of the total process.

Recommendations, Findings, and Alternatives

• *Contextual Determination of Needs.* Determination of the data requirements of state land use planning programs must begin with a thorough analysis of the scope and content of the activities to be undertaken at the state level, by other levels of government, and by the private sector. The planning process and implementing procedures to be used must be developed in enough depth that the information needed to conduct the program can be determined. Without this frame of reference, data needs will quickly become unmanageable and can easily absorb all of the staff, financial, and other resources available to carry out the entire program.

• *Relevance of Data.* Procedures for collecting and storing data must also be realistic in terms of their ability to produce current information, when it is needed, at a level of accuracy and detail consistent with the problem to be addressed or the decision to be made. Systems which are too cumbersome to be used, more detailed than is necessary, and too complex to permit updating will cause resources to be diverted to inventory and storage activities at the expense of other phases of the program.

• *Flexibility of Data Systems.* The data collection program must be structured to accommodate growing and changing needs. Data requirements are both circular and cumulative. Goals and policies for the development and use of land must address the significant problems of the real world. These can only be identified and measured through valid and current information. The planning and regulatory activities designed to achieve land use goals and policies will in turn require further data. The resources available will seldom if ever be adequate to permit finding out in advance everything that might some day need to be known about what might conceivably be involved in a land use program.

• *Federal Involvement.* A data support system utilizing the existing data collection and storage activities of the federal government should be initiated as soon as possible. Any effective state approach to land use planning and regulation will require substantial quantities of data. Critical areas techniques and other implementing procedures will require a much higher quality of information than has generally characterized land use planning efforts in the past. Federal support to the States in meeting these needs is essential since 21 or more States have already initiated land use programs and more are considering doing so. This system should be a joint state-federal operation, conducted on a regional basis.

• *Regional Data Centers.* A state-federal data support system should be organized jointly by the users and the producers of data, using existing resources and statutory authority. The system should be set up on a regional basis, using the standard federal regions or some other logical grouping of States. The sponsorship of the Federal Regional Councils or other interstate agencies would be very helpful in initiating the operation and in securing the cooperation of the federal agencies which conduct data programs. A committee of the state and federal participants should supervise the operation of each center.

• *Principles and Operations of Regional Centers.* The data support system should operate through regional referral and technical assistance centers which function as contact points and expediters between data users and data collectors. The centers would receive requests for information from state land use agencies and others concerned, consolidate these where possible, and bring the users together with the most appropriate federal data sources. They would assist States and other planning agencies in developing land use planning programs by providing information on the availability of data and their capabilities and limitations. The centers would also analyze those data requirements which cannot be met by any existing federal data program and, if sufficiently important, encourage an appropriate federal agency to add this area to an existing activity or develop a new source. Over a period of time the regional centers should acquire and store the most frequently used data and develop electronic data processing capabilities for access to central data files.

The activities of the regional data centers should follow the following priorities:

(a) Identify, locate, and make available data which is most urgently needed to support state, regional, and local land use and resources management programs;

(b) Prepare or disseminate national and multistate regional forecasts of population, employment, and other factors which are an essential part of the framework for land use decisions, under safeguards which prohibit making use of such forecasts mandatory for any purpose;

(c) Identify and acquire other data which are essential to state land use and resource management activities, but which are not provided through any existing federal program;

(d) Search out and incorporate all of the remaining information which can be obtained from existing federal programs but which is beyond the minimum essential needs covered by priority (a) above;

(e) Develop and share software models to facilitate the use of information (e.g., land development, carrying capacity, social and economic impact models).

At all levels and steps in the data collection, storage, retrieval, and interpretation process, there must be adequate safeguards to insure privacy and the security of confidential information. However, security and confidentiality must be balanced against the right of public access.

• *Need for Data Classification System.* Land use and land characteristic classification systems must be devised which satisfy both primary and secondary uses of information. Primary uses include all those which contribute directly to analysis, plan formulation, and regulation, while secondary uses include public information, market analysis by private developers, etc. The differing needs for data for planning and regulation will have to be taken into account, particularly where local governments will be implementing state or regional policies. The different characteristics that describe land use, such as the activity type, intensity of the use, ownership, condition of the land in both natural and man-made aspects, and structure type and status will have to be taken into account, although these obviously cannot be combined into a single classification system.

• *Structure of Data Classification System.* A widely applicable, if not universal, system of classifying natural resource and land use information for use at all governmental levels must incorporate multiple levels of categorization which are collapsible from detailed to general forms. Both the *Standard Land Use Coding Manual* (4 levels)[52] and the *Land Use Classification System for Use with Remote Sensor Data* (2 levels)[53] are this type of system. These two systems differ in the orientation (urban land uses v. natural resources and land cover as a surrogate for activity) and are geared to different collection techniques, but they provide a basis for development of a system which can meet the needs outlined above. Such a system could be developed by merging the two schemes referred to above, using the *Land Use Classification System for Use with Remote Sensor Data* as the basic or framework system at the first two levels, and the *Standard Land Use Coding Manual* to provide greater detail, particularly for urban land uses, at the third and subsequent levels. A committee of current and potential users, university researchers, and others concerned should be organized to develop the combined system and insure that the needs of the maximum number of present and future users are met.

• *Recognition of the Limitations of Data.* Future federal legislation affecting land use or assisting state programs in this field should recognize the uses and limitations of data and its purposes in the planning process. Specification of a long list of mandatory inventories or other data activities at either the state or federal levels will not contribute to the development of land use programs which meet the needs of each State. Extensive rosters of required inventories are bound to result in many States collecting and filing data which is not used in the State's land use program, at a substantial expenditure of time and funds, solely to comply with a federal requirement.

Appendices

Appendix 1

An Allocation of Activities to Levels of Government for Land Use Planning

State level	Local and regional levels	Federal level
Policy Formulation and Enabling Legislation		
Assess problems of growth and development. Evaluate alternatives. Establish state policies for growth and land use; monitor and revise as necessary.	Establish policies for growth and development within the framework of state policies and plans; monitor and revise as necessary.	Establish national growth policy. Formulate national land use policy based on state recommendations and other inputs. Monitor and revise as necessary.
Prepare and enact legislation or amend existing legislation authorizing local governments and/or regional bodies to plan for and regulate land use and development within framework of state policy and program; structure local/regional programs to manage resources in accordance with their capabilities and limitations.		
Determine appropriate levels (state, local, or regional) for conduct of planning and implementing programs.		
Continuously evaluate program performance and consistency with state growth and land use policies.		
Land Use Planning Process		
Develop a process appropriate to the situation in each State. This may range in scope and depth from preparation of statewide development plans, land use allocations, and implementing procedures to designation of areas and activities for planning and regulation by local governments.	Establish and conduct land use program in accordance with state enabling legislation and regulations.	Identify and designate areas and activities of more than state concern.
Select types of areas to be covered by process: entire State, critical areas, key facilities, large-scale development, etc.	Exercise original jurisdiction (permit authority) for state and local programs.	Prepare plans for use and development of federal lands, in consultation with state and local/regional planning agencies and governing bodies.

Identify areas subject to process (if less than entire State) through a systematic procedure for definition, classification, evaluation of importance or priority, and designation.

Set standards and criteria for use or development of designated areas and activities; monitor implementation by local and regional levels and conduct appeals procedure, or regulate directly.

Formulate plans and implementing regulations for areas and activities not covered by local programs.

Program Operation

Establish mechanisms for participation by state agencies, local governments and/or regional bodies, and others concerned.

Establish procedures and standards for public participation at the state and local/regional levels and monitor compliance.

Establish or select mechanisms for identifying and dealing with areas and problems of interstate concern.

Conduct data collection, storage, analysis, and exchange activities required to carry out state program and to support local/regional and interstate programs.

Coordinate state activities which have a significant effect on land use with program:

(1) Functional planning, facility development, and programmatic activities.

(2) Regulation of air, water, noise, and other forms of pollution.

(3) Resource management programs: coastal zone, watershed, soil conservation, etc.

Develop and conduct appeals procedure for local programs.

Assist in identification of areas and activities included in state programs.

Establish mechanisms for participation by local and regional planning, program, and operating agencies, and others concerned.

Establish procedures for public participation which meet state requirements and monitor compliance.

Conduct data collection, storage, analysis, and exchange activities required to support local/regional planning and regulatory program in accordance with standard procedures and classifications.

Coordinate local/regional activities which have a significant effect on land use with program.

Cooperate with state and local/regional planning agencies in their preparation of land use plans for areas which affect federal lands.

Establish mechanisms for participation by federal agencies, public interest groups, and others concerned.

Encourage state and local/regional land use programs through financial support, technical assistance, and other means.

Assist States to develop mechanisms for handling issues of interstate concern.

Cooperate with States in formulating standards and procedures for collection and classification of data.

Bring federal and federally assisted or licensed development activities or land use into conformance with state and local/regional land use programs to the maximum extent consistent with the national interest.

Make surplus federal lands available for use by others in conformance with state and local/regional programs.

The conditions and assumptions summarized in the preceding table provide a basis for outlining the allocation of functions to various levels of government for state land management programs. Their model must be general, since options are open to States in several key areas, but the major elements can be identified with enough precision to illustrate the kinds and amounts of information which are required to support effective state growth policy and land management.

The distribution of functions outlined lists major activities in three broad categories:

(1) Policy formulation and enabling legislation;
(2) The land use planning process; and
(3) Program operation.

Important functions are outlined at three levels: state, local and substate regional, and federal. Local governments and substate regional agencies are combined in a single level since those activities which have the most significant implications for state land use programs are essentially similar at this level. An infinite number of variations and alternatives can be hypothesized to this model, and numerous refinements are required of each of the activities listed at any level.

The model illustrates the mechanics of a state land use program which minimizes state involvement. In this model local governments and/or regional agencies would prepare and implement land use plans much as they have done or have been authorized to do in the past. Applications for permits for use or development of land, or for the kinds of actions conventionally regulated by zoning ordinances, building and housing codes, subdivision regulations, and official maps would be directed to the local or regional office responsible, which would continue to administer local or regional plans and implementing regulations. Appeals from determinations made under these plans and regulations would continue to be handled at the local or regional level. At the same time, local and regional program administrators would be required to observe and enforce those state standards and criteria which would apply in each instance.

In critical areas, these might be detailed and stringent. In other areas, they might be general, and provide advice or guidance. Appeals from determinations based on state land use program requirements would be handled through a procedure operated at the state level to insure uniform application and interpretation and adherence to the intent of state growth and land use policies, when regulations must be modified to resolve specific problems. Reservation of authority by the State to review and change local land use decisions which are not compatible with the State's goals and objectives, and to exercise original jurisdiction in situations where local governments either do not or cannot act, is consistent with these approaches.

The State faces several substantive requirements in this approach, in addition to operating an appeals procedure: formulating and applying growth and land use policies, identifying and regulating areas of particular concern, supervising local or regional implementation of state programs, and conducting local-level programs for those areas where local governments have not acted or regional bodies have not been organized are among the more important state activities.

To meet these responsibilities, the State must engage in an intensive, but broad-scale, resources management process. The data required to conduct this process extend across the full range of social, economic, and physical considerations.

The federal role should incorporate several principles: (1) recognition of the States as the primary authority for land use planning and regulation, (2) a basic orientation to planning as a continuing process containing elements common to all States, (3) concern for effective implementation of the policies and regulations which emerge from this process and for consistency of actions across areas which are divided by political jurisdiction or ownership, and (4) support of the process through financial assistance, provision of essential information, and bringing federal actions which significantly affect land use into conformance with state and local land use programs whenever possible.

Appendix 2

Policy Statement
National Governors' Conference
Sixty-Sixth Annual Meeting
Seattle, Washington
June 1974

State Land Use Planning

There is a need to face the issue of national and statewide land use planning and decision-making in this decade. The proliferating transportation systems, large-scale industrial and economic growth, conflicts in emerging patterns of land use, the fragmentation of governmental entities exercising land use planning powers, and the increased size, scale and impact of private actions have created a situation in which land use management decisions of national, regional and statewide concern are being made on the basis of expediency, tradition, and short-term economic considerations and other factors which are often unrelated to the real concerns of a sound land use policy.

Across the Nation, a failure to conduct sound land use planning has required public and private enterprise to delay, litigate, and cancel proposed public utility and industrial and commercial developments because of unresolved land use questions, thereby causing an unnecessary waste of human and economic resources and a threat to public services, often resulting in decisions to locate utilities and industrial and commercial activities in the area of least public and political resistance, but without regard to relevant environmental and economic considerations.

The land use decisions of the federal government often have a tremendous impact upon the environment and the pattern of development in local communities. The substance and nature of a national land use policy should be formulated upon the expression of the needs and interests of state, regional, and local government, as well as those of the federal government. Federal land use programs should recognize that the long-range resolution of land use matters lies in a significantly increased participation of state government in land management policies and programs.

There should be undertaken the development of a national policy, to be known as the National Land Use Policy, which shall incorporate environmental, economic, social and other appropriate factors. Such policy shall serve as a guide in making specific decisions at the national level which affect the pattern of environmental and industrial growth and development on the federal lands, and shall provide a framework for development of interstate, state, and local land use policy.

The National Land Use Policy should:

A. Foster the continued economic growth of all States and regions of the United States in a manner which is compatible with a quality environment and consistent with other public and private rights.

B. Favor patterns of land use planning, management and development which offer a range of alternative locations for specific activities and encourage the wise and balanced use of the Nation's land and water resources.

C. Favorably influence patterns of population distribution in a manner such that a wide range of scenic environmental and cultural amenities are available to the American people.

D. Contribute to carrying out the federal responsibility for revitalizing existing rural communities and encourage, where appropriate, new communities which offer diverse opportunities and diversity of living styles.

E. Assist state government to assume responsibility for major land use planning and management decisions which are of regional, interstate and national concern.

F. Facilitate increased coordination in the administration of federal programs so as to encourage desirable patterns of environmental, recreational and industrial land use planning.

G. Systematize methods for the exchange of land use, environmental and economic information in order to assist all levels of government in the development and implementation of the National Land Use Policy.

H. Insure that the continuing land use planning process provides a definite linkage between the planning of both private and public lands, especially in those States where an intermingled pattern of federal and non-federal lands exists. There must be an effective and reasonable procedure for the States to interact at an early stage in federal decisions in order to avoid inconsistencies with approved statewide plans and programs.

I. Insure that federal urban and metropolitan programs and activities be consistent with approved statewide land use plans and programs.

J. Provide adequate grant assistance to States to facilitate implementation of the preceding objectives (including the training of qualified land use planners, which would alleviate the prevailing shortage of such).

K. Refrain from the imposition of economic sanctions against States which are unable to comply with federal land use policy requirements. Because of the highly sensitive nature of land use control, major accommodations will have to be made between state and local governments before such controls can be exercised equitably and judiciously. Furthermore, sanctions generally have proved an ineffective tool in bringing about desired change. In this instance, they would be even less likely to be effective since they focus on the Governor alone when it is the equal responsibility of state legislatures and local government officials to develop the joint relationships necessary for exercising land use control. In the effort to bring about this necessary congruence of public and private interests, major emphasis must be placed on educating the public to its desirability.

L. Encourage States to regain their sovereign responsibilities for the protection of critical environmental areas and for assuring that adequate developmental standards and guidelines are enacted at all levels of government.

Intelligent land use planning and management provide the single most important institutional device for preserving and enhancing the environment and for maintaining conditions capable of supporting a quality of life while providing the material means necessary to improve the national standard of living.

Appendix 3

Policy Statement
National Legislative Conference
Intergovernmental Relations Committee
Washington, D.C.
August 1974

Land Use Planning

Land use planning is hardly a new function of government; indeed, there is evidence of it in this country as far back as the late 1600's. But it is coming in for renewed emphasis and in a new perspective with today's increasing awareness of environmental considerations.

Land use planning is the key to environmental management and provides the wherewithal to assure the wisest use of our resources and the most efficient means of guiding growth for the mutual good of all citizens.

The Intergovernmental Relations Committee of the National Legislative Conference believes that the planning process should involve, in appropriate degree and with regard to applicable lands, all levels of government and cooperation among separate agencies within the same level of government.

The Committee recommends that federal legislation should set broad national policy and should encourage and assist the States to prepare and implement land use programs for the protection of areas of critical environmental concern and the control and direction of growth and development of more than local significance.

The Committee further urges that each State should:

1. Set policy and establish guidelines for land use within its borders, with particular emphasis on environmental considerations and balanced usage;

2. Direct the implementation of comprehensive local and regional substate land use plans in conformance with such guidelines;

3. Reserve for itself direct determination of land use only in instances which it deems of impact or importance beyond the scope of a single locality to determine;

4. Set policy with regard to the creation of new communities;

5. Review its existing legislation affecting development patterns to manage the growth that must occur in the manner which shall be consistent with environmental quality.

Appendix 4

Policy Statement
National Association of Attorneys General
1974 Winter Meeting
Hot Springs, Arkansas
December 1974

Land Use Legislation Resolution

WHEREAS, the land resources of the United States are not indestructible and without limit, and

WHEREAS, as our nation's population increases the demands upon our land become greater, and

WHEREAS, land use patterns in our nation have, for a large part, been developed in an unplanned, uncoordinated and uncontrolled manner, and

WHEREAS, such land use patterns are, far too often, destructive of needed environmental natural values and essential ecological relationships and are otherwise not suitable to satisfy the needs of the people of the United States, and

WHEREAS, proper land use management in the long run not only enhances economic productivity and stability, but promotes energy conservation and the control of pollution, and

WHEREAS, the Congress of the United States is now considering various proposals pertaining to land use policy, planning and regulation, and

WHEREAS, a few States have enacted comprehensive land use policy and planning statutes and a larger number of States are considering proposals dealing with the same subject.

NOW, THEREFORE, BE IT RESOLVED as the position of the National Association of Attorneys General that:

1. The National Association of Attorneys General supports the enactment of federal legislation which:
   a. Encourages States and their subdivisions to establish comprehensive land policy and planning programs, while recognizing that primary responsibility for doing so rests with the States and their subdivisions, by providing grants of moneys to these governments to support such endeavors, and
   b. Promotes federal land management policy for federal lands and projects which is compatible with and recognizes that primary responsibility rests with the States and their subdivisions for developing policies and implementing programs, and
2. The National Association of Attorneys General further supports the enactment by each State of comprehensive land policy and planning programs which:
   a. Recognize the historical role of local governments as the primary

implementors of such programs,

b. Take into account and recognize the legitimate statewide, interstate and national interests in such programs, and

c. Develop a governmental planning and decision making process for lands which utilize the best talents of the State and local governments, in a balanced manner, so as to achieve well reasoned policies and decisions pertaining to the protection of the public interest and general welfare.

Footnotes

1. Senate Report Number 93-197, "Land Use Policy and Planning Assistance Act" (Washington, D.C.: U.S. Government Printing Office, 1973), p. 72.

2. Marion Clawson, "Historical Overview of Land-Use Planning in the United States," *Environment: A New Focus for Land Use Planning,* ed. Donald M. McAllister (Washington, D.C.: National Science Foundation, 1973), p. 25.

3. Ibid., p. 28.

4. Senate Report Number 93-197, "Land Use Policy," p. 75.

5. Ibid., p. 78.

6. Office of Management and Budget, *The Catalog of Federal Domestic Assistance* (Washington, D.C.: U.S. Government Printing Office, 1973).

7. The Task Force on Land Use and Urban Growth, *The Use of Land: A Citizen's Policy Guide to Urban Growth,* ed. William K. Reilly (New York: Thomas Y. Crowell Company, 1973), p. 33.

8. Fred Bosselman, David Callies, and John Banta, *The Taking Issue* (Washington, D.C.: U.S. Government Printing Office, 1973), p. 328.

9. Ibid., pp. 236-317.

10. H. M. and Dr. J. W. Patton, "Harbingers of State Growth Policies," *State Government,* Vol. XLVII, No. 2 (Spring 1974), pp. 76-77.

11. *A Legislator's Guide to Land Management* (Lexington, Kentucky: The Council of State Governments, December 1974), pp. 55-57.

12. P.L. 83-560 (1954).

13. P.L. 92-419 (1972).

14. Title V, P.L. 92-419 (1972).

15. *Federal Register,* Vol. 38, No. 201, p. 29022.

16. P.L. 92-583 (1972).

17. Ibid., Sec. 303.

18. *Federal Register,* Vol. 38, No. 299 (November 29, 1973), pp. 33044-51.

19. P.L. 92-500 (1972).

20. 42 U.S.C. 1857; 49 U.S.C. 1421, 1430 (1970).

21. Council on Environmental Quality, *Environmental Quality,* fourth annual report (Washington, D.C.: U.S. Government Printing Office, 1973), p. 168.

22. David E. Gushee, *Federal Water Pollution Control Act Amendments of 1972* (Washington, D.C.: Water Pollution Control Federation, 1973), pp. 5-6.

23. Council on Environmental Quality, *Environmental Quality,* pp. 155-56.

24. P.L. 92-574 (1972).

25. House of Representatives, *1969 Listing of Operating Federal Assistance Programs Compiled during the Roth Study,* 91st Congress, 1st Session, House document No. 91-177 (Washington, D.C.: U.S. Government Printing Office, 1969), pp. 1079-80.

26. *Hunter v. Pittsburg,* 207 U.S. 161, 178-79 (1907).

27. Robert A. Walker, *The Planning Function in Urban Government* (Chicago: University of Chicago).

28. Robert P. Dolan, *Fundamentals of Home Rule* (Kingston, R.I.: Bureau of Government Research, University of Rhode Island, 1960), p. 3.

29. Ibid., p. 3.

30. Donald J. Bogue, *Population Growth in Standard Metropolitan Areas, 1900-1950* (Washington, D.C.: U.S. Government Printing Office, 1953), pp. 9, 13.

31. Title 23 U.S.C., Sec. 134.

32. Bureau of Public Roads, U.S. Department of Commerce, "Urban Transportation Planning," Instructional Memorandum 50-2-63(1) (September 13, 1963).

33. Senate Report Number 93-197, "Land Use Policy," p. 65.

34. "The Big Cypress Conservation Act of 1973," Sec. 380.055(1) (1973).

35. Phyllis Meyers, *Slow Start in Paradise* (Washington, D.C.: The Conservation Foundation, 1974), p. 22.

36. Virginia Curtis (ed.), *Land Use and the Environment*, An Anthology of Readings (Chicago: American Society of Planning Officials, 1973), p. 93.

37. American Law Institute, *A Model Land Development Code*, Tentative draft Number 3 (Philadelphia: 1971), p. 5.

38. Senate Report Number 93-197, "Land Use Policy," p. 128.

39. Hale W. Jenkins, and others, *Areas of Critical Environmental Concern*, Preliminary Report to the Office of the Chief of Engineers, Department of the Army (Smithsonian Institution, 1973), pp. 14-15.

40. Fred Bosselman and others, *The Taking Issue*, pp. 238-55 and 302-9.

41. This overview is adapted from a paper prepared by Dr. Jon A. Kussler for the National Symposium on Resource and Land Information, Reston, Virginia, November 7-9, 1973. The symposium proceedings, *Land Use Management: Proceedings of the National Symposium on Resource and Land Information*, have been published by the Council of State Governments.

42. "Curriculum Essay on Citizens, Politics, and Administration in Urban Neighborhoods," *Public Administration Review*, Vol. XXXII (October 1972), p. 662.

43. *A Legislator's Guide*, pp. 55-57.

44. Phyllis Meyers, *Slow Start in Paradise* (Washington, D.C.: The Conservation Foundation, 1974), p. 25.

45. Philip H. Lewis, Jr., "An Earth-Aid Program — Systems and Methods for Land Resource Policy Development," a paper prepared for the National Conference on Land Policy, Harrisburg, Pa. (June 29-30, 1972), pp. 28-34.

46. Linda S. Corby and Frank S. So, "Annual ASPO School Survey," *Planning*, Vol. 40, No. 1 (January 1974), pp. 20-25.

47. Section 136(b) of the Highway Act of 1970 and Federal Highway Administration Policy and Procedure Memorandum 90-4.

48. Philip H. Lewis, Jr., "An Earth-Aid Program," pp. 24-25.

49. James Anderson and others, "Conference Committee Reports-Data," *Environment: A New Focus for Land Use Planning*, ed. Donald M. McAllister (Washington, D.C.: National Science Foundation, 1973), p. 301.

50. Ibid., pp. 301-2.

51. E. Charles Palmer and Richard Witmer, "Summary Report on Present Capability of States to Generate Land Use Information," a paper prepared for the U.S. Geological Survey Geographic Applications Program (1974).

52. Harold A. Merrill and Jacob Silver, *Standard Land Use Coding Manual* (Washington, D.C.: U.S. Government Printing Office, 1965).

53. James R. Anderson, Ernest E. Hardy and John T. Roach, *A Land Use Classification System for Use with Remote Sensor Data*, Geological Survey Circular 671 (Washington, D.C.: U.S. Government Printing Office, 1972).